TOXIC *Friends*

A Practical Guide to Recognizing and
Dealing with an Unhealthy Friendship

TOXIC Friends

A Practical Guide to Recognizing and Dealing with an Unhealthy Friendship

Foxglove Publications
P.O. Box 252212
6725 Daly Road
West Bloomfield, MI 48322 U.S.A
Orders: www.toxicfriendships.org

First Edition
ISBN 978-0-615-32938-3
Library of Congress Control Number: 2010927178

A Practical Guide to Recognizing and Dealing with an Unhealthy Friendship

Foxglove Publications
West Bloomfield, Michigan

LORAINE SMITH-HINES

In memory of my beloved
cousin and friend,
Mallory

Contents

Acknowledgements

This book would have never come to pass without the help and support of various individuals.

I am indebted to more than 2800 women who shared their toxic friendship stories with me via personal interviews, emails, and/or by completing one of my Toxic Friendship Surveys.

I am especially grateful for my *"therapists on the go"*, as I like to call them. Thanks for listening, not judging, and providing hope and encouragement when I needed it the most.

To my dearest and truest friend Lorraine McKnight; thank you for a healthy and happy friendship of almost thirty years.

Most of all, I want to thank my husband—Linardo—for your emotional support, encouragement, patience, and understanding and my children — Kevin, Tiffany, and Christopher for putting up with me during the writing and rewriting of this book.

And to everyone who assisted in the production of this book, Thank You for your expertise.

Editorial Services: Robin Quinn, www.writingandediting.biz

Cover and Interior Design: James Arneson Art and Design

Thanks to you all, my vision is now a reality.

Warning - Disclaimer

This book is designed to provide information about toxic friendships. It is sold with the understanding that the author and publisher are not engaged in rendering professional mental health services of any kind. If professional help is required, the services of a competent mental health professional should be sought.

The author and Foxglove Publications shall have neither liability nor responsibility for any broken friendship or any emotional damage caused, or alleged to have been caused, directly or indirectly by the information contained in this book.

If you do not wish to be bound by this Warning-Disclaimer, you may return this book to the publisher for a full refund.

A Note from the Author

The purpose of this book is to educate those who seek knowledge and understanding about the nature of toxic friendships and the negative impacts they have on the lives of those who fall prey to them. It is not intended to mend or break up anyone's relationship. It is my intent that after reading this book, you will be able to recognize what a toxic friendship is and be empowered to take control over it in any way you see fit for your individual circumstances.

It is not my purpose to reprint all the information that is available on the subject of toxic friendships, but rather to provide you with a comprehensive guide that should be used in conjunction with other books, articles, manuals, etc. You are encouraged to read all the available information on toxic friendships so that you can make well-informed and educated decisions about how to recognize these relationships, deal with them, eliminate them from your life, or avoid them altogether. A very thorough Glossary is provided in this book to help you understand relevant terms that might be unfamiliar to you.

Many steps have been taken to make sure that the information contained in this book is as complete and accurate as possible; however, there may be typographical as well content mistakes. Therefore, this book should only be used as a general guide and not as the ultimate source of information about toxic friendships.

In addition, the quotes in this book are from original research conducted by myself in the form of personal interviews, emails, or surveys. They are reprinted verbatim and if necessary, excerpted or edited for sense or clarification. As I respect the anonymity of all research participants as well as others, fictitious names have been used to protect the identity of all parties and great care has been taken to preserve the integrity of each example.

Introduction

This book will not focus on my own personal experiences with toxic friends. Still, I do feel that it's necessary to provide a little background on one particular relationship I had as it will help you understand why I chose to write this book.

When I was forty two years old I became the victim of a toxic friendship. My *former toxic friend* or FTF had literally studied me from afar for an entire year without my knowledge after I began circulating in her social network. She had exhibited the behaviors of a predator stalking its prey - just waiting for the right moment to attack. And after waiting patiently for an entire year, the perfect attack moment *finally* came for my FTF. She was in desperate need to fill her friendship gap after her best friend (at that time) had backed away from the friendship with her. This appeared to be the perfect time to *attack* and *invade* my world and so she did.

On the day I met my FTF, she and I talked for several hours as it seemed we had much in common. She asked a lot of personal questions *(a red flag)* which really irritated me. I brought it to her attention and she justified *(a red flag)* such questioning as being something that she did on her job. But that wasn't the real reason for asking me all those personal questions. I later learned that her initial goal was to find out who I was and what my interests were as quickly as possible so that she could find a way to connect with me.

And so the pursuit of my friendship began…

The day after I met my FTF, she earnestly pursued my friendship *(a red flag)* by asking me to engage in some of the activities that I had indicated I had an interest in. But for weeks, I politely declined all invitations and requests because I really didn't want to be bothered nor did I have the time. Besides, I had inklings that something wasn't right with her but I couldn't pinpoint what it was. And after weeks of successfully declining all of her attempts to befriend me, I finally *gave* in. Having closed my business for the summer, I had some extra time on my hands so I started thinking, "*How bad could a friendship with her be?*" After all, we had so much in common (or so I thought) and she *seemed* like a really nice person.

Giving in to her requests to befriend me was the biggest mistake I could have ever made!

~

After connecting with my FTF, my life changed forever. I quickly became the latest victim on her long list of unhealthy friendships (most of which had failed in the long run). The negative experiences I had with my FTF included the *many ways* she took advantage of my kindness, how she constantly *used me*, her *always needing my help*, *lying to me*, and *betraying my trust* (just to name a few).

At one point I was so convinced that there was something wrong with me and that maybe I was overreacting to my FTF's negative behaviors.

Meanwhile; according to her, I had become the one who had "*put up*" with her for the longest period of time. And at that point, I felt like her *best fool* rather than her *best friend*. The record for remaining in a close friendship with her had not surpassed one year; that was, until I entered the picture. My toxic friendship actually lasted a little over two years because I was determined not to become a statistic on her list of failed friendships; so I tried really hard to make ours work. In hindsight, I realize that I should have taken my proper place on that list earlier. But I was the friend who could *change* her toxic behaviors - or so I thought. As result of my naïve thinking, I failed to achieve such an impossible task.

Her previously close friends had backed away and learned to be just casual friends with her and that became my intent as well ...

Trying to change the level and status of my relationship with my FTF was indeed a very slow weaning process; after all, you don't go from being best friends to casual friends overnight. During this weaning process, my FTF ultimately crossed the *"line of no return."* After that happened, there was absolutely no way I could continue to be friends with her on any level. During that tumultuous time in my life, one of the greatest lessons I learned came from one of my FTF's other friends (now a friend of mine). That lesson was that sometimes you have to *walk away* and *stay away* from the things and people you love. Then you can love them at a distance.

That's what I did...

My toxic friendship ironically ended just as it had begun. My FTF once again exhibited the behaviors of a predator stalking its prey after I indicated my intentions to end the friendship. She wouldn't leave me alone. She called me constantly, begging me to remain friends with her. She left crazy voice messages because I wouldn't answer my phone. She sent emails in hopes that I would reply. She would come to my home uninvited but I wouldn't answer the door. Then she started to drive by my house during the times she knew I would be coming and going. So I altered those times. I would go certain places and she would appear minutes later at the same place. I tried really hard to ignore her behaviors and pretend as if she didn't exist but she just wouldn't stop. Eventually I completely removed myself from her social network. That's when my healing process began.

Was walking away easy?

No, it wasn't. But it was the best thing for me to do.

I have yet to look back....

My negative experience with my FTF had a profound impact on my life. It inspired me to learn as much as I could about how and why a friend could treat another friend in such a way and then share that knowledge with others. I had never experienced such a stressful friendship, and as I began my research for this book, I learned that what I experienced with my FTF was not really a *friendship* but rather a very *toxic connection*. I wasn't a friend to her. I was just a human commodity used to fulfill her wants and needs. My research also helped me to understand some of the reasons why my FTF behaved the way that she did and that I couldn't change her negative behaviors no matter how hard I tried. Most importantly, I learned that it was imperative that I regain control of my life no matter how painful the process would be.

If you are trapped within the confines of a toxic friendship wondering whether or not you should end it, that's up to you. I can't tell you to walk away from your toxic friendship. That's your decision. However, what I can do is tell you to educate yourself and learn all that you can about toxic friendships so that you can make educated decisions in regards to your own.

Whatever you decide to do, keep this in mind ... *some friendships are worth keeping; others aren't.*

And, there is life after a toxic friendship.

THE NATURE OF A HEALTHY FRIENDSHIP

Reality *Check*

If you feel you have a healthy friendship, embrace it at this time in your life. Do everything you can to nurture it and maintain its current status. But keep in mind that healthy friendships can run their course and turn toxic at any time.

What is Friendship?

Friendship can be defined as a co-operative and supportive relationship between two or more people. It is a relationship like any other that involves mutual trust, affection, esteem, understanding, respect, and reciprocity. Friends like having each other's company as they often have similar tastes, interests, or beliefs and therefore they share mutually enjoyable activities. Friends offer love and support in times of crisis or need by exchanging advice or showing empathy for one's obstacles or hardships.

Characteristics of a Healthy Friendship

The characteristics of a healthy friendship may seem quite obvious to many. However, some people often get blindsided by the excuses and justifications that toxic friends use in an effort to draw attention away from their negative behaviors. Therefore, many victims become complacent with their friend's ill-treatment of them and consider it *normal* friendship behavior. But healthy friendships don't make you feel unhappy, depressed, angry, etc.

And they don't stress you out or cause you to feel doubtful and/ or confused on a regular or consistent basis.

The characteristics of a healthy friendship are easy to identify. Think about your friendship and use the following indicators as guidelines for helping you determine the quality of your relationship. Use the following acronym to help you remember the characteristics:

THANKS FRIEND

Trust	**F**reedom
Honesty	**R**espect
Acceptance	**I**nspiration
"**N**o" Ability	**E**mpathy
Kindness	**N**egotiation
Sharing	**D**edication

Let's take a closer look at each of these characteristics.

Trust

Trust in a friendship allows you to share your secrets and confidences without fear of betrayal or exploitation. Your personal information is held with the utmost privacy and protection.

Honesty

The truth can be freely spoken without fear of reprimand or retaliation. Neither party takes offense or becomes defensive towards the other when hearing the truth.

Acceptance

The two of you accept each other for who each of you are without judgment or criticism. You both understand that acceptance is not a guarantee of continued friendship.

"No" Ability

There is a mutual understanding that "No" means "No" and that it's OK for friends to say "No" to one another without any repercussions. Both of you understand that choosing not to do something and/or disagreeing with the other is perfectly OK.

Kindness

There is no abuse of each other's kindness. This kindness is evident in the compassion, thoughtfulness, gentleness, and thankfulness displayed in the friendship.

Sharing

Each person takes a shared responsibility for maintaining a healthy and happy friendship. Reciprocity reigns and both friends learn from each other. You spend time doing things that each of you enjoy.

Freedom

There is a mutual understanding that each of you needs personal time and space. The friendship doesn't dominate your time or energy. And it doesn't interfere with your personal affairs or compromise your other relationships and obligations.

Respect

There is a mutual respect for each other's decisions, views, opinions, privacy, etc. Disagreements can occur without put-downs, threats, or repercussions. You don't feel obligated to expose every detail of your life. Spoken and unspoken boundaries of friendship are encouraged and respected.

Inspiration

You feel good about yourself when you are with your friend. Each person encourages the other to pursue her dreams, goals, desires, and aspirations without casting doubts, put-downs, or criticism. Advice is given sparingly and taken when only when necessary.

Empathy

Mutual empathy and compassion for one another is apparent. You understand your friend's pain and she understands yours. She listens with not only her ears but with her heart as well.

Negotiation

There is always "give and take" in the friendship. It's not her way or no way – or vice versa. If there is disagreement, the two of you always find a way to "work it out" so that no one is left with the short end of the stick.

Dedication

Your friend is there for you through thick and thin – and vice versa. She always has your back. She is very devoted to maintaining a healthy relationship and not breaking the unspoken "Rules of Friendship."

Now think about it…

If your friend exhibits these characteristics, there's a good chance that she is truly a good friend and you have a healthy friendship. This may be hard to conceive if you're involved in a toxic friendship. But it's true, healthy and fulfilling friendships have all of these characteristics and then some. If you know of someone who has a genuinely healthy friendship, take some time to talk to her to discover what makes that friendship a successful and happy one.

These are just some of the possible characteristics identified in healthy friendships, as there are many more. But if your friendship is void of any one of the listed characteristics, chances are that it's teetering on the brink of toxicity. And you might want to take some time to reevaluate it.

Benefits of a Healthy Friendship

A healthy friendship can have a positive impact on your life in many different ways. It can make you feel good about life in general because of all the love, support, patience, understanding, and other fringe benefits that it offers.

Healthy friendships don't drive you crazy or stress you out. Instead, they lift up your spirits, while generating great joy, pleasure, enthusiasm, and excitement. You look forward to spending time with your friend because you enjoy and cherish her company.

Myths about Healthy Friendships

- They will last *forever*, no matter what.
- They will *never* turn toxic.
- The friend in the healthy friendship is *always* your best friend.
- You must see, visit, or call your friend *every* day.
- You must *always* assist your friend whenever she asks or needs help.
- You should *never* tell your friend "No".
- You must *always* be at your friend's beck and call or vice versa.
- Your friend needs to know *all* of your secrets and personal business.
- You must *never* speak the truth to your friend if it will hurt her feelings.
- Your kids have to be friends with your friend's kids if they are the same age and/or gender.
- It's *always* OK for your friend to come over to your home unannounced or uninvited.
- The two of you must do *everything* together.
- Friends must *always* agree on everything.
- There must *always* be a dominant friend in the friendship.

Unfortunately, these types of thoughts and behaviors occur in many relationships; thus, some people believe that they are good indicators of a healthy friendship. But they can often lead to conflict, misunderstanding, and a lot of unmet expectations between friends. Therefore, both parties in a friendship must understand that these are just myths. They are not *mandatory* friendship thoughts or behaviors.

Self-Evaluation

Think about any healthy friendships you have or may have had in the past.

List the factors that make or made them successful and happy friendships.

_____

_____

_____

_____

_____

Are any of those factors present in your toxic friendship?

- ○ Yes
- ○ No
- ○ Not Sure

If yes, which ones? List them in the space below.

_____

_____

_____

_____

_____

Chapter 2

THE NATURE OF A TOXIC FRIENDSHIP

Reality Check

It's easy to mistake a toxic friendship for a healthy one if you don't know the difference between the two. Don't beat yourself down the first time you get duped by a toxic friend. Use the negative experience as a learning tool so that you won't get duped a second time around.

What Is a Toxic Friendship?

A toxic friendship is an unhealthy relationship capable of bringing forth an onslaught of negative feelings, emotions, and behaviors. A friendship of this type can be hazardous to your emotional, physical, financial, and spiritual well-being. Toxic friendships lack reciprocity. And they are unbalanced with one friend always giving more than the other or getting the short end of the friendship stick.

Portrait of a Toxic Friend

A toxic friend, also known as the *perpetrator*, is generally a person who wreaks havoc in your life by sending you (the *victim)* on an emotional roller-coaster ride and constantly stressing you out. A toxic friend can be many different things to many different people. Therefore, what is considered toxic to one person may not be considered toxic by others. It's all very personal.

Some toxic friends are cruel, selfish, manipulative, and unkind in one way or another while others are envious, critical, and unsupportive. Other toxic friends are freeloaders who could easily earn reputations for being great takers and poor givers. They may use you as a means of helping themselves to fulfill their own personal wants, needs, and goals while they abuse the friendship and drain the life out of you.

Perpetrators often characterize a good friendship as one in which you cater to their egos and are available at their beck and call 24/7. Some may be unreliable, untrustworthy, and quite comfortable with making promises that they have no means or intentions of keeping.

Forty-year-old Candace wrote this about her toxic friendship of two years:

> *Something just feels out-of-whack with her. I can't quite put my finger on it. She has lied to me and manipulated me in the past. When I was angry at her for these actions, I had to listen to how unfair I was being, and how much I had hurt her with my anger and by not talking to her. The fact was that I felt so hurt and betrayed by what she had done that I couldn't talk to her about it at the time. I would have spoken to her sooner, but she wouldn't give me any time to deal with my feelings. I received emails and phone calls all threatening to end the friendship if I didn't answer her by a specific date. This just made me more upset. When I finally did tell her how I felt, she admitted to lying to me and manipulating the issue. Over the next six months, I was told every two weeks or so about how much I had hurt her, and how betrayed she felt, and how she couldn't trust me. Not to mention that what she had previously admitted to supposedly hadn't even happened according to her. It became just a slight exaggeration. But there was no mention of my hurt and disappointment. And there's also this suspicion I have that she actually gets some kind of enjoyment out of my pain. I can't quite nail it down; it's just this sense that she doesn't really want good things for me. I still question what has happened and hope it's not all in my head.*

There's just this sense of something not being right. She makes me feel like I don't trust myself and like I don't want to hurt her. I don't want to leave her with no one because she's in the middle of a separation. So now I really feel that I can't walk out. She's always demanded some kind of verbal affirmation, or promises of eternal friendship, but everything in me just wants to shut down.

Although Candice was unable to pinpoint why she felt the way she did about her friendship, she knew something was not right. Her intuition alerted her to the fact that her friendship might be in danger and that the conflict with her friend was causing her to lose sight of herself.

Impacts of a Toxic Friendship

Toxic friendships can have a negative impact on your life in many different ways. They can cause conflict or disruption in your family, career, finances, relationships with others, etc. They can stifle your dreams and aspirations, crush your self-esteem, and cause you to lose sight of yourself.

Here's what twenty-year-old Katy had to say about her toxic friend:

Her emotional instability, how she would blame me when I wasn't able to make her feel better, her selfishness, and lack of respect for me … it all made me question her as a friend. She would forget our arguments after a minute; meanwhile, I would stew about it for hours and sometimes days. And then she'd blame me and say that I held grudges and that I get mad over nothing. I would often try to talk seriously about something that was bothering me and she would act stupidly and childishly and make jokes. It makes me feel trapped and doomed. When I think of leaving her, I feel a horrible, gnawing guilt to the point where I am unable to function and focus on other things. I feel insecure and I start to feel convinced that I'm at fault, not her, and that something must *be wrong <u>with me</u>. I feel depressed, rejected, and ashamed that I could let this happen. I also feel incredibly angry and resentful. I bottled up a lot of my feelings because she would constantly criticize my complaints and say that I was getting mad over nothing. I constantly questioned myself, and after a few years, it became almost impossible to speak out at all, for fear of her criticism. I am currently deciding how to end the friendship ... it's difficult.*

As you can see, a toxic friendship has a way of infecting your life to the point where you don't recognize or even accept the toxic behaviors as being what they really are until it is too late. That is when you realize how much drama and trauma you have endured all for the sake of an unhealthy friendship.

Toxic friendships can cause you to question your own sanity and second-guess the reality that is often overshadowed by the subtle deception and manipulation that frequently occurs in such relationships. Therefore, it's very important to pay close attention to those feelings of *"something not being right"* about your friend or the friendship. If you suspect that your friendship may be toxic or unhealthy in one way or another, use the following test to deny or confirm your suspicions.

Toxic Friendship Test

Use the following test to assess or confirm your suspicions of having a toxic friendship.

1. After spending time with my friend or talking to her on the telephone, I often feel stressed, drained, angry, belittled, sad, or a host of other negative feelings and emotions.

☐ Yes	☐ No	☐ Sometimes	☐ N/A

2. There is little or no reciprocity in this friendship. It is very unequal, and I'm always giving while my friend is always taking.

☐ Yes	☐ No	☐ Sometimes	☐ N/A

3. My friend criticizes and puts me down but she really doesn't mean any harm because that's just how she is.

☐ Yes	☐ No	☐ Sometimes	☐ N/A

4. My friend is very selfish and only cares about herself and her feelings, not mine.

☐ Yes	☐ No	☐ Sometimes	☐ N/A

5. When I have a conversation with my friend, the topic of discussion is almost always about her. Then when I change the subject to talk about myself, she conveniently remembers that she has something else to do.

☐ Yes	☐ No	☐ Sometimes	☐ N/A

6. My friend wants to know all of my business but will not share hers with me.

☐ Yes	☐ No	☐ Sometimes	☐ N/A

7. I put up with a lot of nonsense from my friend because she has a lot of personal issues. She's always under a lot of stress.

☐ Yes	☐ No	☐ Sometimes	☐ N/A

8. My friend uses me as a verbal punching bag when she's having a bad day because she knows I will always bounce back from her blows.

☐ Yes	☐ No	☐ Sometimes	☐ N/A

9. My friend uses me and takes advantage of my kindness.

☐ Yes	☐ No	☐ Sometimes	☐ N/A

10. I always support my friend but she doesn't do the same for me.

☐ Yes	☐ No	☐ Sometimes	☐ N/A

11. My friend talks too much so my secrets are not safe with her.

☐ Yes	☐ No	☐ Sometimes	☐ N/A

12. When I hang out with my friend, we always go where she wants to go and shop where she wants to shop.

☐ Yes	☐ No	☐ Sometimes	☐ N/A

13. I try really hard to keep the peace with my friend even though she constantly irritates me and gets on my last nerve.

☐ Yes	☐ No	☐ Sometimes	☐ N/A

14. The bad times outweigh the good times that I have with my friend.

☐ Yes	☐ No	☐ Sometimes	☐ N/A

15. My friend thinks she's "better" than me so she treats me like crap and tries to embarrass me in front of other people.

| ☐ Yes | ☐ No | ☐ Sometimes | ☐ N/A |

16. My friend is always flirting with or trying to come between me and my significant other.

| ☐ Yes | ☐ No | ☐ Sometimes | ☐ N/A |

17. My friend is jealous of me and my accomplishments and tries to put me down or criticize me whenever I achieve another success.

| ☐ Yes | ☐ No | ☐ Sometimes | ☐ N/A |

18. My friend is very lonely and tries to dominate all of my time so I can spend it with her.

| ☐ Yes | ☐ No | ☐ Sometimes | ☐ N/A |

19. My friend is always borrowing money from me and never paying it back.

| ☐ Yes | ☐ No | ☐ Sometimes | ☐ N/A |

20. My friend lacks empathy. When I tell her how much she hurts me, she turns on a deaf ear and tells me I'm too sensitive or overreacting.

| ☐ Yes | ☐ No | ☐ Sometimes | ☐ N/A |

What Your Answers Mean

- If you answered "Yes" to most of the questions, chances are you have a toxic friendship.
- If you answered "Sometimes" to most of the questions, you might want to make some changes in your friendship because it could be headed down the road to toxicity.
- If you answered "No" to most of the questions, chances are your friendship might be considered a healthy one. Good for you!

Note: This test only identifies a few of the behaviors that could indicate a toxic friendship. There are certainly many others that can be considered toxic. As I mentioned earlier, what's considered toxic by one person may not be to another. So evaluate your own situation.

Levels of Toxic Friendships

The degree of negativity a toxic friendship has on you depends on the level of intimacy between you and your friend. For instance, a relationship with a toxic casual friend may not affect you as much as one with a best or closely bonded friend.

Toxic Casual Friend: The behaviors of a Toxic Casual Friend are less likely to get under your skin. She is annoying and irritating to say the least but there's no emotional bond, connection, or intimacy. Her behaviors are often acknowledged but then ignored because you know she is only likely to be in your presence for just a short time. You can take her or leave her, and your contact and communication with her are kept at a bare minimum. She has no friendship privileges or benefits.

Toxic Close Friend: The Toxic Close Friend is a step above the Toxic Casual Friend. There is an obvious connection and an emerging emotional bond. However, due to her numerous exhibitions of toxic behaviors, she has yet to cross the line of becoming your true *best friend.* This type of toxic friend has limited friendship privileges and benefits.

Toxic Best Friend: The Toxic Best Friend knows everything there is to know about you and vice versa. She is the one you can call your second self, the one you may have a remarkable history with. There is a strong emotional bond, and she is the closest and dearest to you. Although you have the highest level of intimacy with this friend, her toxic behaviors make the friendship unbearable most of time. Nevertheless, she has full friendship benefits and privileges.

How would you classify your level of friendship with your toxic friend?

- O Casual
- O Close
- O Best

Has the level changed during the course of the friendship?

- O Yes
- O No
- O Not Sure

Keep in mind that no matter what the level of intimacy is, toxic friendships are unhealthy and unsatisfying. However, because of the human need for companionship, victims often remain trapped within the emotional confines of such relationships. They also remain trapped for various *other* reasons – many of which will be discussed later in this book.

Self-Evaluation

Think about your toxic friendship ...

List the factors that make your friendship a toxic or unhealthy one.

_____

_____

_____

_____

_____

Compare this list to the list you made of the things that were present in your healthy friendships in Chapter 1.

Then take some time to honestly answer the following questions about your friendship ...

Do the positive things in your friendship outweigh the negative things or do the negative things outweigh the positive things?

_____

_____

_____

_____

_____

Are you acknowledging the real truth about your friendship?
- ○ Yes
- ○ No
- ○ Sometimes

THE FRIENEMIES

Reality *Check*

The love you have for your frienemy can destroy you – but so can the hate.

What Is a Frienemy?

Now that you know the characteristics of a healthy friendship as well as a toxic one, some of you are probably thinking that your friend has the characteristics of both. This is certainly the case with what can be called a "frienemy," and relationships with frienemies create "frienemy-ships," not friendships.

A frienemy is the friend you love and hate at the same time. She brings joy and pain, as well as hope and despair – sometimes all in the same minute, hour, and day. She can be any one or a combination of various types of toxic friends; however, at times, she *can* and *is* the epitome of a good friend. Unfortunately, there lies the problem for many. She is a good friend at any given moment in your life, but your worst enemy in the next … your frienemy.

Sometimes frienemies are hard to spot in the beginning. My advice… If you have a gut instinct that causes you to question the relationship, don't hesitate to follow it. Heed the warning.

Friend or Enemy?

Types of Frienemies

Wannabe

This type of frienemy starts off being the very best friend you will ever want to have – or so you think. But as time passes, you will discover that she has very low self-esteem and feels less than perfect in comparison to you. This type of self-loathing manifests itself in her covert jealousy and envious behaviors. Her devious behavior may not be directed at you, but perhaps your job, family, or significant other as she tries to steal those things away from you.

Opportunist

This type of frienemy blatantly takes advantage of you and your misfortunes, and she is often allowed to do so because of the perceived bond that has developed between the two of you. The love that you have for this friend makes you easy prey to her underhanded and less than friendly acts. Although she may appear to be standing by your side through the difficult times in your life, she is actually calculating the ways in which she can benefit from your misfortunes.

Mesmerizer

These types of frienemies are like trophy friends; they are charming, fun, and interesting. They may have value in the beginning of the relationship but as time passes you begin to lose interest in them as you realize that much of who they appear to be is only a facade. However, even though your interest wanes, you still may find it difficult to remove them completely from your life. Because despite the things you dislike about them, there is always some miniscule thing that you do like which is often used as an excuse to hold on to the unhealthy relationship.

Backstabber

This type of frienemy will stab you in the back and act as if there's nothing wrong with what she did. She will constantly say one thing to you in private but will quickly change the whole scenario in the presence of a group of people. The Backstabber has no qualms about talking negatively about you and putting you down when you are not present, and she will deny any such accusations when confronted with the truth.

Facts about Frienemies

- She is really an enemy disguised as a friend.
- She will always offer a listening ear but it's only to gather all the details about any drama or conflict you may have in your life so that she can use them against you on an "as needed" basis.
- She is generally a *good* person but you can always count on her to bring you down in one way or another.
- She is nice one day and nasty the next.
- She will stand by your side but there is always a hefty price to pay.
- She does favors for you but only if it will benefit herself as well.
- She laughs and grins in your face but has no qualms about stabbing you in the back.
- She treats everyone like a close friend and uses any information gained from them as a weapon of emotional mass destruction.

- You usually get the short end of the stick or you are the one left holding the bag when things go wrong.
- She professes to you and others that the two of you are *best friends,* but her actions generally prove otherwise after she gets what she wants from you.
- She is an unnecessary and sometimes defiant competitor against you.
- She tries to make herself look good in the eyes of everyone else while making you look like the bad one.
- She has little or no empathy in regards to your feelings, losses, or concerns.

These are just a few facts about frienemies, there are indeed many more.

Frienemy-ships

A frienemy-ship is the unhealthy relationship, connection, or bond one develops with a frienemy. We often unconsciously refer to our relationships with frienemies as *friendships* for the lack of a better term. But frienemy-ships are only synonymous to friendships in that they are relationships based on many factors that draw the two parties towards one another.

Use the following test to help determine whether or not your relationship is a *friendship* or *frienemy-ship.*

Friend versus Frienemy Test

1. Do you have a love/hate type of relationship with your friend in question?

☐ Yes	☐ No	☐ Sometimes	☐ N/A

2. Do you trust your friend?

☐ Yes	☐ No	☐ Sometimes	☐ N/A

3. Does your friend show a false sense of caring towards you?

| ☐ Yes | ☐ No | ☐ Sometimes | ☐ N/A |

4. Does she try to gain personal information about you while neglecting to share her own personal information with you?

| ☐ Yes | ☐ No | ☐ Sometimes | ☐ N/A |

5. Do you think and/or talk negatively about your friend when she is not in your presence?

| ☐ Yes | ☐ No | ☐ Sometimes | ☐ N/A |

6. Do you act less than the person you truly are when you are in the company of your friend?

| ☐ Yes | ☐ No | ☐ Sometimes | ☐ N/A |

7. Does she bring out the worst in you when the two of you get together?

| ☐ Yes | ☐ No | ☐ Sometimes | ☐ N/A |

8. Do you feel like you are in a competition when she discusses work, children, hobbies, finances, significant other, accomplishments, etc.?

| ☐ Yes | ☐ No | ☐ Sometimes | ☐ N/A |

9. Does your friend have a pattern of building you up and then letting you down?

| ☐ Yes | ☐ No | ☐ Sometimes | ☐ N/A |

10. Does your relationship with the friend in question compare to your relationships with others whom you consider to be true friends?

☐ Yes	☐ No	☐ Sometimes	☐ N/A

11. Does she constantly use passive aggressive type behaviors in an effort to manipulate you?

☐ Yes	☐ No	☐ Sometimes	☐ N/A

12. Do you often feel like your friend plays emotional games with you?

☐ Yes	☐ No	☐ Sometimes	☐ N/A

13. Do your instincts tell you that she is jealous and envious of many aspects of your life but not all?

☐ Yes	☐ No	☐ Sometimes	☐ N/A

14. Does she constantly brag to you about how good her relationships are with her *other* friends?

☐ Yes	☐ No	☐ Sometimes	☐ N/A

15. Does your friend give praise for your successes and accomplishments but at the same time resents them and nitpicks to finds flaws and failures in them?

☐ Yes	☐ No	☐ Sometimes	☐ N/A

16. Does she use excessive flattery by constantly complimenting you but at the same time copies your style and tries to outdo you?

☐ Yes	☐ No	☐ Sometimes	☐ N/A

17. Do you cringe when she opens her mouth to speak?

☐ Yes	☐ No	☐ Sometimes	☐ N/A

18. Do you dread and regret the time you spend with her?

☐ Yes	☐ No	☐ Sometimes	☐ N/A

19. Does she broadcast your most covenant and personal secrets to others after you've told her not to?

☐ Yes	☐ No	☐ Sometimes	☐ N/A

20. Does she frequently put you down and/or snub you in a *nice* way?

☐ Yes	☐ No	☐ Sometimes	☐ N/A

What Your Answers Mean

- If you answered "Yes" to most of the questions, chances are that your so-called "friend" is not a friend but a frienemy instead.
- If you answered "Sometimes" to most of the questions, the status of your relationship is more than likely in jeopardy and could easily cross over to becoming a frienemy-ship.
- If you answered "No" to most of the questions, chances are your relationship might actually be a *true* friendship.

Note: Frienemies can be hard to spot because most of the time they have just as many good qualities as they do bad ones. It's not unusual to have a love/hate relationship with them because they will often share the same interests and values as you do. This makes it difficult to classify them as being just an enemy and to ultimately move them to your list of toxic friends.

Why Frienemy-ships Are Toxic

Frienemy-ships can be hazardous to you because they cause blind-spots and can impair your ability to recognize healthy friendships. They wreck havoc on your emotional, physical, financial, mental, and spiritual well-being in many different ways, just like toxic friendships do. However, unlike many toxic friendships, you may actually like your frienemy for as many reasons as you dislike her. This can stand in the way of you seeing the real truth about the relationship.

Self-Evaluation

Think about it … is the person you call *friend*, really a friend or is she a frienemy?

- ◯ Friend
- ◯ Frienemy
- ◯ Not Sure Yet

If you think your *relationship* is a frienemy-ship, use the space below to list the reasons why you feel this way.

_____

_____

_____

_____

_____

RED FLAGS OF A TOXIC FRIENDSHIP

Reality *Check*

Sometimes it is difficult to know whether or not a seemingly healthy friendship is toxic or turning toxic if you are not familiar with the red flags and warning signs.

What Are Red Flags?

A red flag is often used as a warning signal for impending danger, and when we encounter one, we know to run for cover or at the very least to back off and proceed with caution. But we cannot run from that which we don't recognize as an immediate danger or threat. And sometimes a dangerous friendship is camouflaged by friendly smiles and false acts of kindness as was the case for thirty-year-old Marge, who described how she became involved with her toxic friend:

> *She asked me to come to her office one night because she felt we had a connection. She said she wanted to be friends but then she started using me immediately. And as soon as I got too close to her, she would push me away and then pull me back in like I was a damn yo-yo! I let her do that until she later told me that the friendship was not about me but about her and her wants and needs. She didn't give a damn about me or my feelings.*

Even though our friends don't walk around waving red flags or carrying warning signs, they often exhibit questionable behaviors and actions that are indicators of their impending toxic behaviors. Marge's friend started using her immediately, but she didn't heed the warning until much later.

Unfortunately, Marge is not alone; many people often ignore the red flags and other warning signs and proceed with cultivating or maintaining toxic friendships. After all, who enters a friendship thinking it will be a toxic one? And don't forget about our human need for companionship; a toxic friend is better than having no friend at all, right? Well, at least it can seem that way in the beginning.

Your friend's behavior might be mistaken for something else besides a red flag. However, if you are forewarned and educated about the red flags, you can train your brain to be on the lookout for any signs of toxicity in your current or future friendships. Then react and deal with them accordingly.

Early Red Flags

In many cases, there are obvious red flags at the beginning of the friendship, but unfortunately people just don't recognize them. However, there are many other cases where the red flags are quite clear and obvious but they're simply ignored as in the case with Catherine. She had hopes that the negative behaviors her friend displayed right away were not what they seemed to be and would just eventually fade away. But they didn't, even after almost twenty years of friendship.

Sixty-year-old Catherine wrote this about her toxic friendship:

> Yes, there were warning signs. She told me she was "silent and deadly." I never thought she would use it against me, and we became inseparable in school and we have also worked together. My friendship has not ended yet, but it may because she's nuts!

Catherine's friend let her know that her own behavior was *deadly* but she did not heed the warning. She continued to cultivate the friendship, and as her friend's behavior got progressively worse, Catherine's tolerance for it became increasingly greater. She began to justify, rationalize, and make excuses for her friend's negative behaviors – which allowed her to continue cultivating a very unhealthy relationship. And even after twenty years of toxicity, the deep emotional bond she developed with her friend keeps her trapped in a toxic friendship as she admitted in the comment about her inability to just simply let it go.

Catherine is not alone in her inability to let go of her toxic friendship. Letting go is often very difficult to do even if the friendship causes great sorrow and pain. That is why it's so important for victims to not be fooled by the wit and charm of the perpetrators in the first place. Once an emotional bond develops, they simply have you hooked. They are good at deceiving anyone who appears to be easy prey.

If your friend exhibits negative behaviors that make you feel uncomfortable or leery at onset of the friendship or any time during it, more than likely those behaviors will continue. And eventually those same negative behaviors will cause you to either end the friendship later on, or in many cases; continue it as you suffer in silence. Heed the warnings and follow your gut instincts. If something doesn't feel right, there's a fairly good chance that it isn't.

Even the smartest and most confident woman can fall prey to the vile behaviors of a toxic friend as twenty-seven-year-old Sidney explained:

> *Everyone told me not to be friends with her. People were saying how she is a user and a bad friend. I didn't listen because I didn't want to follow the crowd and I felt that she was very misunderstood. So I decided to give the friendship a try, but that ended up being a very big mistake on my part. I have many regrets now.*

Why not follow the crowd sometimes? Many victims are so naive that they want their friendships to be the epitome of Gayle

& Oprah's. They often don't enter into new friendships thinking they could be toxic connections. Instead, many women are on the never-ending search for their new *best friend forever* or BFF. So they not only ignore the early red flags and warning signs that show themselves, they also ignore the warnings from those who may have been victimized by the perpetrator or observed her toxic behaviors first-hand.

Eighteen-year-old Kelly explains how she was duped by a toxic friend because she chose to ignore the obvious warning signs:

> *She would always try to keep me away from my other friends and even my boyfriend. She would always have some excuse to be in-between my other friendships and I always just figured it was nothing. Eventually I saw who she really was, but this happened too late because she had already taken so much away from me. I couldn't believe what I allowed her to do to me. I should have known better. Everyone who knew me could not believe that I allowed her to do all the bad things that she did. It was unbelievable, but I can guarantee that I won't ever get tricked like this again.*

The reality is that most of us just like Kelly, do know better but at the same time we don't want to think the worst of our friendships. After all, it is our human desire to want the companionship of others no matter what the cost. So we often just carry on with unhealthy friendships and accept our friends' toxic behaviors as *business as usual.* We often settle with their bad way of being a *friend.*

Again, we all need some type of human companionship. But if we educate ourselves about what is and what isn't a healthy friendship, we will all be less likely to be victimized, hypnotized, or brainwashed by the deceptive acts of the perpetrator. Knowledge is power and the key to helping us understand the difference between a healthy relationship and a toxic one.

Red Flags Checklist

The following is a general list of red flags, warning signs, and characteristic behaviors that you should pay close attention to and not accept as *healthy* friendship behavior. Keep in mind that this is not an inclusive list. There are numerous others based on the type of toxic friend you have and, of course, your own individual circumstances. The important thing to do is to pay attention to any behaviors that consistently cause you to experience an onslaught of negative feelings and emotions. Ignoring your feelings could be detrimental to your emotional, physical, financial, mental, and spiritual well-being.

Check all those that apply to your friendship.

- ○ Criticizes, belittles, or puts you down in very subtle ways.
- ○ Constantly lies to you, twists the truth, or runs from the truth.
- ○ Makes promises that she has no intentions of keeping.
- ○ Makes excuses for her ill-treatment of you.
- ○ Wants and/or demands all of your time and energy.
- ○ Has a history of failed friendships and changes friends frequently.
- ○ Very nosy and interferes with your personal business.
- ○ Asks for your help and advice frequently and excessively.
- ○ She is very needy, clingy, and dependent on you.
- ○ Has issues/drama with one of her other friends.
- ○ She is extremely jealous of you and your accomplishments.
- ○ Tries to make you feel bad about your appearance.
- ○ She was unusually and excessively nice to you when you first met her.
- ○ Acts fake or phony or pretends to be something she's not.
- ○ Demands frequent contact and communication with you.
- ○ Has issues/drama with a spouse or significant other.
- ○ She has low self-esteem, self-confidence, or self-worth.
- ○ Is domineering and tries to control you and the friendship.

○ Engages in illegal activities and tries to get you involved.
○ Blames you for all the negative things that happen to her.
○ Talks negatively to you about her other friends.
○ Uses friends to validate who she is as a person.
○ Takes advantage of you and uses you big time.
○ Doesn't care about your feelings or concerns, only cares about self.
○ Borrows money or possessions from you and never returns them, and then has many excuses as to why she doesn't.

Remember, these are just a few of the red flags of a toxic friendship. It's better to be cautious rather than careless in your observations of a friend's questionable or negative behaviors, actions, as well as her reactions. And keep this in mind; what's considered toxic to you may not be considered toxic to someone else, but that doesn't lessen the toxicity of your own friendship. Do not allow others to manipulate your feelings or emotions by telling you that you are just overreacting to your friend's negative behaviors and ill-treatment of you. Remember it's all very personal.

Ignored Red Flags

Many victims of toxic friendships may not recognize their relationships as being toxic right away because they ignore the obvious red flags and warning signs. They may only have inklings that something is just not right with the perpetrator.

Victims may not always be able to put their finger on it, but what they do know with no uncertainty is that their friendship does not make them feel good. They may often feel uncomfortable, agitated, angry, scared, confused, or even frustrated when they spend time with their friend. And oftentimes, a simple conversation with the perpetrator can send the victim over the edge or on an emotional roller-coaster ride. But for various reasons, many victims become accustomed to their friend's way of being a *friend* and begin to accept, justify, or rationalize their toxic behaviors in public. However, in private, victims suffer in silence as they try to figure out what went wrong with the friendship and whether or not it's their own fault.

Results from the short survey showed that many victims recognized their friendships were toxic early on; nevertheless, they ignored the red flags and proceeded with *cultivating* their toxic friendships.

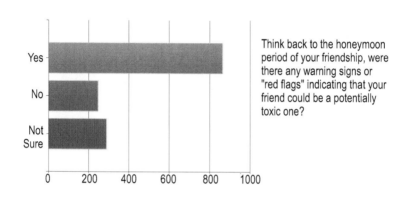

Think back to the honeymoon period of your friendship, were there any warning signs or "red flags" indicating that your friend could be a potentially toxic one?

And for various reasons (discussed later in Chapter 8), a very large number of victims chose to *remain* in their toxic friendships even though they knew they were unhealthy for them.

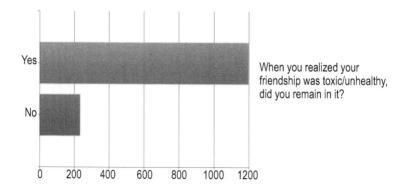

When you realized your friendship was toxic/unhealthy, did you remain in it?

Survey Questions & Answers

If you have the slightest inkling that your friendship is toxic or you already know for sure, don't hesitate to take some type of action. Not doing so could be detrimental to your physical, mental, financial, and spiritual well-being, as the victims below discovered.

Survey Question: *Thinking back to the honeymoon period of your friendship, were there any warning signs or red flags indicating that your friend could be a potentially toxic one?*

Responses:

Over half of the respondents answered "Yes" to this question but many others answered "No" or indicated that they were unsure as to whether or not their toxic friend exhibited any red flags or warning signs.

Survey Question: *If yes, briefly explain what the warning signs were.*

Responses:

She was overly critical, controlling, and easily hurt by me, but had a double standard for her behavior ...

The constant name-calling, control issues, competitiveness, temper tantrums when things don't go her way ...

There were constant snippy little comments intended to make me feel bad about myself and several occasions where I would be out having a good time, but she would have some drama that I'd have to drop everything for ...

Her accusations, blaming, not listening, putting responsibility on me that was not mine to take, and her judging and insulting me ...

She had sex with a man I was dating, but denied understanding the situation ...

Fractious relationships with other friends, dropped friends, no close female friends, backbiting ...

Pinching my arm out of frustration, yelling at me, telling me how I should behave ...

Her constant lying and deception ...

Her anger and need for revenge ...

The constant drama in her life was never-ending and that's all she ever talked about, everything was about her ...

She was always being negative, never happy, and always down in the dumps about one thing or another ...

The drug addiction, neediness, lying to others, catching her in lies to me, using others for personal gratification, lots of excuses in taking no responsibility for actions, lots of problems ...

Her sarcasm, cruelty, and jealousy towards me ...

Always comparing my level of faith to hers and tried to make me feel guilty about my blessings because I didn't go to church as often as she did ...

She would tell my personal business to others ...

Her hot and cold behavior towards me, one minute very loving and intense, then the next turning it around that I was too intense and telling me to fuck off and get away from her ...

Constantly borrowing money, and never paying it back. Only calling when wanting something ...

She is very needy and clingy, and she calls me four times a day ...

She wanted to spend all of her time with me and didn't like any of my dates ...

The attention issues, she was putting more demands on me than my boyfriend/husband at the time ...

These are just a sampling of the red flags that victims ignored.

Self-Evaluation

Every toxic friendship has red flags that are often ignored for one reason or another. Think about your friendship …

What red flags or warning signs have you chosen to ignore? List them in the space below.

_____

_____

_____

_____

_____

TYPES OF TOXIC FRIENDS

Reality *Check*

Don't waste your time or energy trying to convince others that you have a toxic friendship. They may never understand how you feel or what you are going through emotionally, financially, mentally, spiritually, physically, or sexually.

Categories of Toxic Friends

There are many different types of toxic friends, each with its own distinct set of red flags, warning signs, and characteristic behaviors. Your friend may have just one or perhaps several of the many different characteristics listed in the previous chapter; however, keep in mind that all it takes is just *one* to be considered toxic. And one is certainly more than enough.

The individual types of toxic friends have each been placed in a category that best describes the nature of their overall toxic behaviors. Some types may overlap in that the type of behavior exhibited can actually place them in one or more categories. I have chosen to place them in the following categories based on the similarities of the behaviors, as well as the negative outcomes and effects of each type as it relates to the victim.

Attention Seekers

Attention Seekers are toxic friends who thrive off the attention of others and generally don't care whether the attention is positive or negative. Of course, they would *prefer* the positive, but most often their behaviors only elicit negative or unfavorable attention from others. Their main objective is to be seen, heard, or acknowledged in one way or another, so they will take the attention as it comes.

Types of Attention Seekers

- ☠ Drama Queen
- ☠ Copycat
- ☠ One-Upper
- ☠ Know-It-All
- ☠ Daredevil

Avoiders

Avoiders are toxic friends who always deliver you the short end of the friendship stick, by wheedling their way out of sticky and uncomfortable situations or avoiding them altogether with their lack of accountability. They always have excuses, rationalizations, or justifications for not living up to their commitments, responsibilities, obligations, etc. – to you or to others.

Types of Avoiders

- ☠ Runner
- ☠ Houdini
- ☠ Procrastinator
- ☠ Sloth

Busy Body Big Mouths

Busy Body Big Mouths are toxic friends who are addicted to running their mouth for one reason or another. They give a new meaning to the phrase *"the gift of gab."* And not only do they possess the gift, they make sure that everyone knows they have it by putting your business in the streets, not minding their own, and driving you crazy with their excessive talking about nothing or something that is totally irrelevant and meaningless to you.

They always have something to say about everything and simply don't know when or how to shut their big mouths.

Types of Busy Body Big Mouths

- ☠ Exposer
- ☠ Talk-a-Holic
- ☠ Interrogator
- ☠ Double Talker

Charlatans

The Charlatans are all about playing and winning the games of deception, games in which no one but themselves want to play. They are masters at the craft of making you believe that they are truly something they are not. Their games of deception are played by their rules and on their turf, where they are always the winner at any physical, emotional, spiritual, or financial cost.

Types of Charlatans

- ☠ Phony
- ☠ Swindler
- ☠ Charmer
- ☠ Liar
- ☠ Hetero-Flexible
- ☠ Religious Hypocrite

Control Freaks

Control Freaks are the toxic friends who like to boss you around, tell you what to do, how to do it, when to do it, and who to do it with. They try to take charge of every aspect of your life. They are manipulative, bossy, critical, demanding, and power hungry. They are self-centered and self-seeking individuals who aren't satisfied unless they are controlling your life or someone else's.

Types of Control Freaks

- ☠ Regulator
- ☠ Abuser

☠ Emotional Bully
☠ Queen Bee
☠ Stalker

Ego Trippers

Ego Trippers are toxic friends who are only concerned about their own well-being and what others can do for them. They are generally selfish and self-seeking individuals, with their major goal in life being to maintain nothing but self. You will forever be an Ego Tripper's best friend if you continually and consistently cater to their every want, need, demand, or desire.

Types of Ego Trippers

☠ Arrogant
☠ Narcissist
☠ Self-Centered
☠ Spoiled Brat

Emotional Manipulators

Emotional Manipulators are toxic friends who like to play mind games. They often cause a lot of emotional hurt, pain, and suffering for the victim. In most cases, they are well aware of their behavior but will deny any accusations that they are messing with your head. Instead, they will put it all on you and make you seem like you're the one with the issues. In reality … they are the crazy ones!

Types of Emotional Manipulators

☠ Guilt Tripper
☠ Misery Magnet
☠ Gas Lighter
☠ Passive Aggressive
☠ Jekyll & Hyde
☠ Injustice Collector

Extremists

Extremists are toxic friends who have a tendency to take things to the extreme – whether it's how they spend their money, how they treat their friends and others, or how they live their lives in general. Every aspect of their life is somehow exaggerated to the point of irritation, frustration, and disgust for those who are involved with them. They usually go far beyond what is reasonable, moderate, normal, acceptable, or comfortable for most people.

Types of Extremists

- ☠ Penny Pincher
- ☠ Addict
- ☠ People Pleaser
- ☠ Grouch
- ☠ Obnoxious
- ☠ Promiscuous
- ☠ Xenophobic

Fault Finders

The Fault Finders are toxic friends who are in a constant mode of frustration and dissatisfaction, and this attitude seems to control every aspect of their life. They constantly complain about you or others, criticize you and your life, and they are always looking for ways to blame you for the shortcomings or negativity in their own lives.

Types of Fault Finders

- ☠ Whiner
- ☠ Complainer
- ☠ Criticizer
- ☠ Accuser
- ☠ Victimized

Heartbreakers

Heartbreakers are the toxic friends who cause deep emotional hurt and pain. They know just how much you love and care about them and often use those things as weapons of manipulation and control. They know what makes you tick; therefore, they know which buttons to push to make you laugh or cry.

Types of Heartbreakers

- ☠ Betrayer
- ☠ Promise Breaker
- ☠ Snubber
- ☠ Cheater
- ☠ Envious
- ☠ Competitor

Leeches

Leeches are the toxic friends who exploit you in one way or another for their own personal gain or advantage. They are mental, physical, and financial freeloaders who have little regard for your feelings or concerns because they're only worried about maintaining self at the expense of others. They latch on to anyone who appears to be easily pulled into their world of "*I need help so please help me.*" They are selfish individuals who always look for the easy way out of anything and everything in life that might require them to take care of or be responsible for their own livelihood and/or well-being.

Types of Leeches

- ☠ User
- ☠ Time Bandit
- ☠ Keeper
- ☠ Rider
- ☠ Lonely
- ☠ Needy

Rescuers

Rescuers are addicted to you and feel that they must be your savior in one way or another. They have a strong sense that you are incapable of living a satisfying and productive life without some type of wanted or unwanted intervention from them. Therefore, their goal in life appears to be making sure you are taken care of by them. However, because they devote so much time trying to coddle you, they often neglect their own needs and ultimately drain the life out of themselves. That's when it becomes apparent that they really have a strong hidden desire to be needed by you.

Types of Rescuers

- ☠ Caretaker
- ☠ Advisor
- ☠ Doctor
- ☠ Defender
- ☠ Problem Solver
- ☠ Interloper

Simpletons

Simpletons often lack common sense along with the ability to say "No," which allows others to easily take advantage of them in more ways than one. They are very naive and easy-going individuals who go with the flow rather than rock the boat. They do not speak up and protect themselves from unwanted actions or requests so the victim usually gets stressed out and frustrated from having to save them from unpleasant situations.

Types of Simpletons

- ☠ Flunky
- ☠ Zombie
- ☠ Sitting Duck
- ☠ Clueless

As you read about the different types of toxic friends, don't forget to evaluate yourself. You might find that you're just as toxic as your friend. You may have become *toxic by association* or you may have already been that way.

List of Toxic Friends

The following list was compiled based on information obtained from research, personal interviews, as well as data from my *Toxic Friendship Surveys*.

1. Abuser
2. Accuser
3. Addict
4. Advisor
5. Arrogant
6. Betrayer
7. Caretaker
8. Charmer
9. Cheater
10. Clueless
11. Competitor
12. Complainer
13. Copycat
14. Criticizer
15. Daredevil
16. Defender
17. Doctor
18. Double Talker
19. Drama Queen
20. Emotional Bully
21. Envious
22. Exposer
23. Flunky
24. Gas Lighter
25. Grouch
26. Guilt Tripper
27. Hetero-Flexible
28. Houdini
29. Injustice Collector
30. Interloper
31. Interrogator
32. Jekyll & Hyde
33. Keeper
34. Know-It-All
35. Liar
36. Lonely
37. Misery Magnet
38. Narcissist
39. Needy
40. Obnoxious
41. One-Upper
42. Passive Aggressive
43. Penny Pincher
44. People Pleaser
45. Phony
46. Problem Solver
47. Procrastinator
48. Promiscuous
49. Promise Breaker
50. Queen Bee
51. Regulator
52. Religious Hypocrite
53. Rider
54. Runner
55. Self-Centered
56. Sitting Duck
57. Sloth
58. Snubber

59. Spoiled Brat
60. Stalker
61. Swindler
62. Talk-a-Holic
63. Time Bandit
65. User
66. Victimized
67. Whiner
68. Xenophobic
68. Zombie

Some survey respondents used the following words to describe their toxic friends:

Copycat, self absorbed, narcissist
Sensitive, pretentious
Liar, cheater
Fault finder, one sided
Self-centered, criticizer, regulator, one-upper
Needy, user
Double crossing, selfish
Betrayer, backstabber
Power hungry, control freak, bully
Pretender, phony
Unreliable, whiner
Lazy, complainer
Manipulative, bossy, abusive
Negative, jealous, possessive, competitive
Passive aggressive, co-dependent
Sexually manipulative, victim
Over-exaggerator, drama queen
Gossiper, loud, curser, busy body
Angry, judgmental
Clingy, intrusive, verbally abusive, demanding
Rude, ignorant, obnoxious

Toxic Friends Behavioral Checklist

Although this book does not give detailed information about the various types of toxic friends and how to deal with each one, the following is a brief description of all of them.

For a more detailed discussion on the various types, read the second, third, and fourth installments of the Toxic Friends book series.

Put a check by those that describe the behavior(s) of your toxic friend.

- ○ **Abuser** – Verbally, physically, emotionally, or sexually abusive.
- ○ **Accuser** – Blames you for all the problems, issues, and drama in her life.
- ○ **Addict** – Dependent on some type of addictive entity.
- ○ **Advisor** – Analyzes everything you do and constantly gives unwanted advice.
- ○ **Arrogant** – Very conceited; has an extremely high level of pride.
- ○ **Betrayer** – Double-crosses you and betrays your trust.
- ○ **Caretaker** – Acts like your parent and has a strong desire to care for you.
- ○ **Charmer** – Very charismatic and presents herself as being a nice person.
- ○ **Cheater** – Flirts, messes around with, or steals your romantic partner.
- ○ **Clueless** – Lacks common sense and the ability to learn things quickly.
- ○ **Competitor** – Defiantly competes against you.
- ○ **Complainer** – Gripes and complains excessively about everything.
- ○ **Copycat** – Imitates and copies everything you do.
- ○ **Criticizer** – Extremely critical and finds fault in everything you do.
- ○ **Daredevil** – Risk taker; does things that put self or others in danger.
- ○ **Defender** – Won't let you fight your own battles.
- ○ **Doctor** – Although not a doctor, tries to diagnose and treat all of your ailments.

○ **Double Talker** – Uses ambiguous language to confuse you.

○ **Drama Queen** – Makes a drama out of every situation in her life.

○ **Emotional Bully** – Uses verbal and emotional abuse to control you.

○ **Envious** – Extremely jealous of you.

○ **Exposer** – Discloses your secrets and confidences.

○ **Flunky** – Acts as a servant to many and does whatever anyone tells her to do.

○ **Gas Lighter** – Psychological abuser who tries to cloud your perception of reality.

○ **Grouch** – Habitually in a bad mood and/or angry about something.

○ **Guilt Tripper** – Tries to make you feel guilty about everything you do or say.

○ **Hetero-Flexible** – Heterosexual but likes the same sex as well.

○ **Houdini** – Very clever at escaping from uncomfortable situations.

○ **Injustice Collector** – Grudge holder who remembers and itemizes every slight.

○ **Interloper** – Selfishly interferes with your life.

○ **Interrogator** – Asks too many personal questions.

○ **Jekyll & Hyde** – Has unpredictable mood swings.

○ **Keeper** – Borrows your stuff and never returns it.

○ **Know-It-All** – Tries to undermine your intelligence.

○ **Liar** – Has trouble telling the truth.

○ **Lonely** – Overly dependent on your companionship.

○ **Misery Magnet** – Very sad and miserable person.

○ **Narcissist** – Loves self and has no care or concern for others.

○ **Needy** – Very clingy and overly dependent on you.

○ **Obnoxious** – Very offensive and unpleasant to be around.

○ **One Upper** – Always trying to be one up on you.

○ **Passive Aggressive** – Uses non-verbal actions to let you know she's angry or upset.

○ **Penny Pincher** – Cheap and thrifty; doesn't like to spend her own money.

○ **People Pleaser** – Always trying to please others while neglecting self.

○ **Phony** – Pretends to be someone or something she's not.

○ **Problem Solver** – Obsessed with solving your problems while ignoring her own.

○ **Procrastinator** – Postpones doing things in a timely manner.

○ **Promiscuous** – Exhibits sexually immoral behavior and/or actions.

○ **Promise Breaker** – Unreliable and undependable; constantly breaks promises.

○ **Queen Bee** – Very bitchy and thinks she's better than everyone else.

○ **Regulator** – Very bossy and demanding; tries to control you.

○ **Religious Hypocrite** – Acts like she's holier than thou.

○ **Rider** – Rides on the coattails of others.

○ **Runner** – Runs from the truth, responsibility, and confrontation.

○ **Self-Centered** – Concerned with her own feelings, wants, needs, and desires.

○ **Sitting Duck** – Constantly victimized by others; target of ridicule or harassment.

○ **Sloth** – Extremely lazy and expects others to do things for her.

○ **Snubber** – Dislikes you and blatantly shuns or rejects you in front of others.

○ **Spoiled Brat** – Selfish and demanding Prima Donna.

○ **Stalker** – Invades your personal space without your permission.

○ **Swindler** – Steals from you by subtle deception.
○ **Talk-a-Holic** – Talks constantly and excessively.
○ **Time Bandit** – Likes to waste your personal time.
○ **User** – Uses you for personal wants and gains.
○ **Victimized** – Blames others for the bad things that happen in her life.
○ **Whiner** – Constantly whines and complains about everything.
○ **Xenophobic** - Has extreme dislike or fear of that which is unknown or different from oneself.
○ **Zombie** – Won't speak up for self and allows others to take advantage of her.

If your friend, especially a new one, is overly and excessively nice to you- proceed with caution. You may not discover what her real motives are until she has you *hooked* on a friendship with her. And by that time, great emotional damage may have already occurred.

If you feel that something is just not right with your friendship, don't ignore your gut feelings. Any delay in accepting what has been revealed to you will no doubt delay and stifle your ability to effectively deal with it or to eliminate it from your life altogether.

Self–Evaluation

We all can be a little toxic at times. However, we might not have the ability to take an objective look at the role we play in our toxic friendships. Whether we are initially the toxic one or whether we become *toxic by association,* we must take responsibility for the role we consciously or unconsciously play in our unhealthy friendships. It is imperative that we monitor and modify our own negative behaviors.

Think about it ... do you exhibit any of the behaviors described above on a *consistent* basis?

○ Yes
○ No
○ Not sure

If you answered, "*Yes*," perhaps you are just as toxic as your friend.

Has anyone ever accused you of causing the conflict or demise of a once valued friendship?

○ Yes
○ No
○ Not sure

Think about your toxic friendship… list any other things you may have done to contribute to the toxicity of the friendship.

_____

_____

_____

_____

_____

A COMMON PHENOMENON

Reality *Check*

Remaining in a toxic friendship can be a vicious cycle that will go on and on until you put an end to it. Haven't you been there and done that … too many times?

If you're currently trapped in a toxic friendship and you feel like no one understands, you're right. Most people do not understand if they have never had a toxic friendship experience. However, if it's any consolation to you … just know that you're not alone. The emotional pain, suffering, drama, and trauma that you're enduring is felt by many others across the globe every single day. So hang in there!

Prevalence of Toxic Friendships

The results from my Toxic Friendship Surveys reveal that toxic friendships affect women of various ages, races, cultures, economic standings, educational levels, and marital statuses, with occurrences spanning across the globe. Before I started writing this book, I had no idea this was such a wide-spread problem. I thought I was the only one living through the madness and nightmare of a toxic friendship. On the contrary, I discovered that I was actually in the minority because at my age, I had never experienced a toxic friendship before. I had managed to avoid any and all contact with toxic friends even as a teenager.

I was surprised to find that there were so many people who had had at least one toxic friendship in their life. Just about everyone I talked to about this subject – including other friends, relatives, and strangers – had experienced one or more toxic friendships, and they were eager to discuss their experiences with me.

My conversations about toxic friendships were nothing people had not heard before, yet most had never used the term *toxic* to describe their friendships. They generally used terms such as "betrayer," "backstabber," "liar," "cheater," etc. to describe the perpetrator. Nevertheless, after I explained the term *toxic* as it relates to friendships, everyone agreed that the friendship they described was indeed a toxic one.

Just like many of you, I thought my experience was unique but it wasn't. And because of my own personal experience and recovery, I can say with great certainty that there is a bright light at the end of the very dark and often lonely tunnel that leads to emotional recovery and toxic friendship freedom as well as self-rediscovery. So once again, I say, "*Hang in there! This too shall pass*".

Why Are There So Many Toxic Friends?

As we live and grow in our lives, we change as do our relationships. We gain more education, increase or sometimes decrease our incomes, our families change, our level of life responsibilities change, we decrease our tolerance for nonsense, we change our lifestyles and interests, etc. However, sometimes those changes are not accepted or understood by the people we call our friends. They may harbor anger, resentment, or jealousy aimed at the changes because of the way in which they impact the friendship. But instead of walking away from a situation that is less appealing or less advantageous to them, they hang on to it – thus perpetuating a toxic/unhealthy friendship and becoming a perpetrator.

But changes in the way you live your life are not the only contributing factors in the high incidences of toxic friendships. There are actually many reasons. Some of the reasons are beyond our personal control but others are not. This book does not go into details about them; however, I do feel it's worth mentioning the reasons why some victims felt their toxic friends exhibited such behaviors.

Here's just a sampling of their reasons:

Her mother passed away when she was young and she had no guidance and I figure the only way she feels she can get ahead is to take advantage of people.

Despite intense talk of how smart, powerful, great, etc. she was, I suspect that she is just grasping out for good, strong people under the assumption that she can control them.

She might just be mean and honestly think bad things about me or she could just be secretly jealous. I don't know though, it might be a little bit of both.

Things are not good in her family dynamics – in certain areas she has lost total control over situations, such as a bullying adolescent grandson who lives with her and her husband, who is a depressive alcoholic.

She knows that I will not fight back unless she pushes just the right buttons.

Her lack of empathy and the inability to realize the affect of her actions on me and if she does realize the affect on me, she doesn't care.

She wants to be "in" with certain people and then her other "friends" she uses. She keeps her friends separated based on need.

I'm not sure, maybe insecurity.

She had really bad acne as a teenager and used to get a hard time from some guys.

She was raised by an alcoholic mother who verbally and physically abused her.

Her insecurity, possibly a personality disorder and I think she was confusing love for me with threat and control. I think there may be a possible lesbian tendency in her.

She was emotionally needy and had unhealthy relationships in her family.

I am not sure. I think she was in an unhappy marriage and I think she thought she was above everyone and the world revolved around her. She was unhappy and going to take it out on everyone and anyone.

Her relationship fell apart and she began a downward spiral, desperate to get back together with her significant other. She adopted his manipulative and abusive tactics toward her own family and friends. She had everything taken from her and became jealous of anyone else who had a relationship and sought to destroy other people's happiness. Misery loves company, is the epitome of her behavior.

She has an alcoholic father and husband, anger issues, financial problems and jealousy towards anyone in a better situation than herself either financially or someone more happy.

I'm thinking it's because she has little self worth so criticizing other people and creating drama provides some kind of remedy for her.

She has a lot of issues that run very deep and they have not been dealt with properly.

She is a heavy cannabis smoker and alcohol drinker – she is likely very insecure and lonely (despite being married) and she thinks it's everyone else's fault that she's like that.

She has a bad background and is socially maladapted.

I can't truly know for certain. But I don't take it personally any longer. I see the same self absorption toward her children – her need of being number one is so extreme that she doesn't even take an interest in her own grandson and resents her children for their relationships with their spouses.

As you will grow to understand more and more, the prevalence of toxic friendships is not only due to the behaviors of the toxic friend but also the actions and reactions displayed by the victims.

The Perpetrator's Role

Inability to Maintain Healthy Relationships

Some people lack the ability to maintain healthy and mean-ingful relationships for one reason or another. So they develop a pattern of changing friends frequently and do not recognize or acknowledge the pattern even when it is brought to their attention. Instead, they blame their friends for their inability to remain in a relationship with them. Toxic friends often push others away by their frequent displays of toxic behaviors, and when they lose one friend, they quickly find another one. They often view friends as simple commodities to be used as needed then discarded and traded for new ones when they no longer fit their friendship mode; thus, they leave behind victim after victim. And all the while, they know that they'll never truly be friendless because their often twisted perception of reality leads them to believe that everyone needs a friend – so why can't it be them?

Undiagnosed Personality or Psychological Problems

There are a lot of adults in our society who have undiagnosed personality disorders, many of which did not manifest until they reached early adulthood. **Narcissistic Personality Disorder** is just one of ten personality disorders described in the American Psychiatric Association's *Diagnostic and Statistical Manual of Mental Disorders (DSM)*. In brief, people with this disorder are self-centered, arrogant, think the world revolves around them, lack empathy, think they are better than others, etc. Those are indeed the characteristic behaviors of several of the toxic friendship types discussed in this book.

In other words, some of our toxic friends have some serious personality deficits and deficiencies which can have negative impacts on their interpersonal relationships, including but not limited to … *friendships*. And these are the people we unknowingly choose and often maintain as toxic friends.

It's a Means to an End

Some people, no matter what, will continue to be toxic. It's a way of life and a means to an end for them. There are people who simply lack empathy and could care less about how bad they make others feel. They see no reason to change their toxic behaviors if doing so will take away their ability to manipulate and control others to get what they want out of life. As long as they can find victims, they will continue to victimize.

The Victim's Role

Need for Companionship

It's not uncommon to see victims trying desperately to maintain a toxic friendship. Fear of being left *friendless* if they end an unhealthy friendship is a great concern for them. They often suffer in silence and put up with their friend's unfriendly behavior, thus perpetuating the toxicity. In their mind, a toxic friend is better than no friend at all.

Personal Ignorance

Some people are so naive that they allow themselves to be mistreated for no reason other than the fact that it is a learned behavior stemming from the way others have treated them in the past. They are accustomed to being treated as a second-class citizen, so it has become a way of life for them. If their *best* friend treats them like crap, what's the big deal? Everyone else treats them that way, so why shouldn't they accept it from the perpetrator? "Besides she doesn't *really* mean harm, that's just the way she is"… is often the victim's way of thinking. And oftentimes, the victims are too blind to see that the perpetrator is a real jerk, so they accept their own personal justifications for their friend's ill treatment of them without any questions asked and no complaints made either to the friend or anyone else. They simply go with the flow of toxicity.

Inability to Free Self

Many victims don't know how to free themselves from a toxic friendship for various reasons. So they remain in it as they wait for the proverbial signs of a healthy friendship to all of a sudden overshadow the toxic ones exhibited consistently by their friend. Some victims even try to change their friend's behavior, not realizing the impossibility of such a task.

In many cases, *Toxic Strongholds* (explained in Chapter 8) keep victims trapped within the confines of a toxic friendship.

Fear Mentality

Many victims are afraid to face the truth about their toxic friendships, while others are afraid to confront their toxic friends about their behaviors. The fear may be fueled by many things, including the fact that the friendship may end because of the truth they reveal. Other victims fear some type of physical or psychological retaliation from the perpetrator. And in some cases, the victims would rather endure their toxic friendships rather than deal with the possible outcome of negative actions and/or reactions from the perpetrator.

Cycle of Toxicity

No matter what the reasons are for the prevalence of toxic friendships, these relationships will continue to exist because of the Cycle of Toxicity that many victims perpetuate.

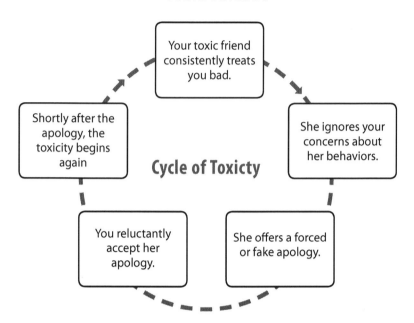

This cycle occurs when ...

- Your friend consistently treats you bad by doing things to hurt you or to make you angry or upset. She sees nothing wrong or inappropriate about her behaviors or actions.

- She ignores your concerns about her ill treatment of you. You try to explain to her how angry or upset you are or how much she has hurt you, but she turns a deaf ear as she tries to justify her behaviors.

- Despite denying her behaviors, she reluctantly apologizes to you and says she will never do *it* again. But that's only after you make a big fuss about it.

- After trying to reason and compromise with the perpetrator, you finally accept her apology in hopes that this time she will actually try to change her negative behavior.

- Shortly afterwards, when your toxic friends thinks you have cooled off, she repeats the same toxic behaviors and thus the cycle begins again.

Toxic Enablers

Toxic enablers are those victims who help perpetuate their friends' toxic behavior(s) in various ways. Some of the behaviors and actions exhibited by toxic enablers are those that they hope will help the perpetrator, but in fact they only enable them to continue their toxic behaviors.

Types of Toxic Enablers

- Justifiers
- Caterers
- Acceptors
- Ignorers
- Duplicators

Justifiers

Justifiers justify the perpetrator's behaviors by making excuses or giving reasons as to why she behaves the way she does. They defend the perpetrator's inappropriate and negative behaviors and will even go as far as to validate what she does. They explain away every negative and ill treatment that the perpetrator dishes out by saying things such as: *"She didn't really mean it," "She had a bad day,"* or *"She just needed to vent,"* plus whatever other excuses they can think of to justify why they allow themselves to remain in such an unhealthy friendship.

Caterers

Caterers cater to the perpetrator's wants and needs, and are available at their beck and call. They answer every call for help and will drop what they're doing to aid the perpetrator. Caterers put off what they need to do for themselves for the perpetrator's sake. They deny their own feelings and concerns while giving their all and personal best to the perpetrator, who will take all that they give and still ask for more. Caterers *like* to give but their giving is often accompanied by complaining. Nevertheless, they keep on giving as long as the perpetrators keep on accepting and taking. Why? Because some don't know how to say "No" and others just don't want to say "No." Doing so would make it seem as if they didn't care about the perpetrator.

Acceptors

A toxic friend is better than no friend at all. That's the motto of the Acceptors. They tolerate the perpetrator's toxic behavior because they feel that if they confront her about it, she will walk away and leave them friendless. The perpetrator's ill-treatment becomes normal and acceptable behavior within the realms of their friendship.

Ignorers

Ignorers passively ignore the perpetrator's negative behaviors, but not because they are trying to prove a point. It's because they fear the response and reactions they will receive if they speak up about it or about their hope that the perpetrator will change.

Duplicators

Duplicators copy the negative behaviors of the perpetrator. In their minds, two wrongs make it right. If the perpetrator treats her unkindly, the Duplicator will treat the perpetrator the same way. And that gives her a sense of vindication and justification. What the Duplicator fails to realize is that this type of behavior on her part leads her to becoming toxic by association.

These are just a few ways that Toxic Enablers help perpetuate the perpetrators toxic behaviors.

Toxic by Association

Everyone is probably familiar with the old saying, *"guilty by association."* For instance, if your friend robs a bank and you drive the getaway car, you are just as guilty of committing a crime as the perpetrator. Try to defend yourself by saying that you didn't rob the bank but your friend did. Your pleas of innocence probably will not matter, but why not? Even though you didn't physically rob the bank, you drove the getaway car. So that makes you *"guilty by association"* in most cases – even if you were unaware of the perpetrator's unlawful plans.

The same holds true for toxic friendships. Whether we choose to believe it or not, we have a tendency to become *toxic by association* if we associate with the toxicity too long. If you find yourself acting, reacting, and responding like your toxic friend or treating others as she treats you, you have become *toxic by association*. The way in which she *is* becomes the way in which you eventually *are* … toxic.

Here's what thirty-seven-year-old Margie had to say about becoming toxic by association:

> *The biggest thing for me, when recognizing that I needed out of this friendship, was when I realized that I started to portray her characteristics in my other friendships and just in life in general. Things that I had always thought badly of her doing, I was now doing the same. I was becoming my environment. When it came time to meet with my ex-friend, I would try to limit any opportunity for her to make a comment about me. I would have to play a role or she would do her best to try to embarrass me in front of others. I was exhausted after our meet-ups and I realized that I was wasting valuable time and missing out on what a real friendship could be.*

Victims may not be willing to admit or take responsibility for their role in their toxic friendships. As mentioned before, it takes two people to maintain an even toxic relationship. You may not have been the cause of the initial toxicity. But if you maintain the status quo, your responses and/or reactions to the perpetrators negative behavior will eventually take its toll on you. And you may find yourself duplicating the same negative behaviors against the perpetrator and/or others in your life.

Self-Esteem and Toxic Friendships

Self-esteem is respect for oneself and confidence in your own merit and abilities. It is belief in your own self-worth as an individual and is not dependent on the validity or confirmation from others. Victims who have a low self-esteem often remain trapped in unhealthy relationships because they don't feel worthy of healthy ones.

A toxic friendship can destroy your self-esteem to the point where you completely lose sight of who you once were before the toxicity entered into your life. And if you entered the toxic friendship with low self-esteem already, chances are that your relationship with the perpetrator will cause you more harm than good.

Self-Esteem Checklist

Perpetrators often victimize others because they themselves suffer from low self-esteem. If you're not sure whether your friend suffers from low self-esteem, use this checklist to confirm or deny your suspicions. (You can also use this list to help you assess the status of your own self-esteem. Just put yourself in each scenario.)

○ Frequently puts down herself and engages in a lot of negative self-talk.
○ She has lots of self-doubts and feelings of hopelessness.
○ Sees herself as a failure and is reluctant to express her own ideas, lacks belief in self.
○ Doesn't feel she's capable of doing anything right.
○ Doesn't care about what she looks like and often neglects her physical appearance.
○ Uses negative terms such as "I can't," "I don't," "I won't," etc.
○ Has no confidence in personal abilities.
○ Allows others to bully or take advantage of her.
○ Believes the negative things that others may say about her.
○ Afraid to try new experiences and changes; lacks trust.
○ Covers up feelings of inadequacy by bragging or exaggerating about her successes or accomplishments.
○ People pleaser, always trying to please others at the expense of neglecting self.

○ Has a strong need for constant support, approval, or validation from others.

○ Lacks accountability; frequently blames others for her personal shortcomings.

○ Constantly focuses on things that happened in the past.

○ Apologizes excessively.

○ Extremely sensitive to criticism.

○ Habitually criticizes and puts down others.

○ Has exaggerated responses to defeats or disappointments; wants to be perfect, but sees self as far from perfect.

○ Acts phony and wastes a lot of time and energy trying to maintain a false image.

○ Doesn't know who she is; low level of self-awareness.

○ Easily embarrassed, humiliated, or devastated by others.

Maintain Your Sanity and Peace of Mind

Whatever the perpetrator's reasons are for being toxic, just remember they are her issues not yours. You must understand that whatever her issues may be, they can and will have a negative impact on your relationship with her.

The perpetrator's behaviors may be learned based on past experiences in her own life. Perhaps she was a victim of verbal or emotional abuse, or maybe she was the neighborhood bully, or the caretaker for everyone she ever crossed paths with.

Maybe none of the above is the cause of your friend's toxic behavior. Some people, for whatever reason(s), like to make the lives of others a living nightmare. Perhaps that is your friend's goal in life ... to make *your* life a living hell just because she can. And if that is the case, there are some important things you should do in order to maintain your own sanity and peace of mind. Here's a few of them:

- *Do not take ownership, blame, or responsibility for her negative behavior; it's not your fault, no matter what she says.*

- *Learn all that you can about toxic friendships because knowledge is power.*
- *Proceed with caution based on your own individual circumstances; sometimes that means completely ending the toxic friendship.*
- *Know that you cannot change your friend, no matter how hard you try; she has to want to make a change and most of the time she won't even acknowledge her negative behaviors.*
- *If you want change, change the way you react and respond to your toxic friend and again … sometimes that simply means walking away and staying away.*

Self-Evaluation

It takes two to "tangle." Think about the things you may have done to perpetuate the toxicity in your friendship. List them in the space below.

_____

_____

_____

_____

If you were unable to think of anything on your own, consider the following:

If you have failed to communicate your true feelings about your friendship to your friend, you have contributed to the toxicity of your friendship …

If you have denied and not accepted the truth about your friendship because you *really* want to make it to work, you have contributed to the toxicity of your friendship …

If you are waiting for the *right* time to tell her the friendship is toxic, you are contributing to the toxicity of your friendship …

If fear has you suffering in silence, you are contributing to the toxicity of your friendship …

GENERAL TIPS FOR DEALING WITH TOXIC FRIENDS

Reality *Check*

However you ultimately decide to deal with your toxic friendship is up to you; a small step is better than no action at all. Take control, and don't allow a toxic friendship to complicate or ruin your life.

There are many things one can do to lessen the negative effects of a toxic friendship, including ending it altogether or finding effective ways of maintaining it. But just as there are many different types of toxic friends, there are also just as many different ways to deal with each variation. The way you deal with one type might prove ineffective when dealing with another kind of toxic friend. However, there are some general things one should always do when dealing with *any and all* types of toxic friends.

Educate Yourself

Knowledge is power. Learn all that you can about toxic friendships. In addition, learn about the various types of personalities and the disorders that plague some of the perpetrators because they can have devastating impacts on their interpersonal relationships with others.

There is always something to learn, even if you think you already know it all. There will always be new sources of information. Still, keep in mind that much of the old information will prove to be just as valuable as it was when you read it the first time.

Sources of information include:

- Books
- Internet
- Magazines
- Articles on the Web
- Counselors or therapists
- Testimonies from victims and/or survivors

Document Your Feelings and Concerns

Use what I like to call a *Journal of Toxicity* or *JOT*. The JOT is a journal that is used strictly for the purpose of writing about your toxic friendship experiences.

Write down how your friendship makes you feel. Include specific examples of the perpetrator's toxic behaviors and the negative effects they have on you and the friendship. This will serve as written proof of her toxicity and as a confirmation of why you need to make some changes in your friendship or end it altogether. Without sharing your JOT with the perpetrator, compile a separate list of your feelings and concerns. Then share them with her with the sole purpose being to make the toxic friend aware of the behaviors and their negative effects, but not to try and change her.

Five Reasons to Keep a JOT

1. It provides a safe place for you to express and clarify your thoughts and feelings about what is happening in your toxic friendship, without fear of criticism, judgment, or reprimand.
2. It allows you to see the truth about your toxic friendship. It can provide you with a clear confirmation and validation of what you've been sensing and experiencing.
3. It gives you the opportunity to gain valuable knowledge about yourself as you document your responses and re-

actions to the perpetrator's behavior and mistreatment of you.

4. It serves as a valuable problem-solving tool as you can write down and keep track of possible solutions or ways to deal with the perpetrator.

5. It gives you an opportunity to release some of the negative feelings and emotions you have, thus decreasing some of the effects of the stress and strain of the toxic friendship.

What to Write in a JOT

That of course, depends on your individual circumstances. However, in general, you should try to include some of the following things.

- **The date and time:** This allows you to reflect and to ask yourself questions, such as: "*Is there a particular time or day that triggers certain reactions from either my friend or myself?*" and "*Are there certain days when I feel worse off than others?*"

- **Your feelings and emotions:** This allows you to process them and release some of the stress you may be feeling.

- **Examples of the perpetrator's toxic behaviors:** This serves as proof and confirmation of her toxicity, and it also provides a written record of such.

- **Examples of how you respond and react to your friend's behavior:** This allows you to assess your own behavior and determine where you need to make changes, if necessary.

- **Ways you might solve your toxic friendship problem, rather than constantly thinking about it.** You can write down your plan of action and revisit or modify it as often as necessary.

- **The progress you make in dealing with the perpetrator.** You can look back through your JOT and track your progress or lack of, whether it's towards improving the friendship or ending it altogether.

- **Ways in which your toxic friendship negatively impacts your life.** Again, this provides a written record for your own personal evaluation and modification.

These are just some general suggestions of what you could write in your JOT. Again, it's all personal and you should write what is relevant to your individual circumstances.

Important Note: Your JOT serves as a Reality Check for you. It allows you to see the real truth about your friendship. At some point and time, you will go back and read your JOT, and you might be surprised at the things you allowed yourself to endure in the name of friendship.

Communicate Your Concerns

Communication is an integral part of any relationship including a friendship. And just as with other relationships, if there is a communication deficit, the relationship is bound to have some issues. Oftentimes, toxic friends are unaware of their toxic behaviors, so it's up to us to bring it to their attention.

Communicate your feelings and concerns but be calm and stay neutral as you confront her. Always use "I" statements. This is about you and how you feel, not about the perpetrator, her reactions, or how bad she may feel afterwards. She may not like what you have to say but that should not stop you from doing what needs to be done.

What the Perpetrator Needs to Know

The Truth

She needs to know the truth about how her behavior impacts your friendship with her. She needs to know your true feelings! You may be afraid to confront your friend just as much as you are afraid of the outcome of her continuous toxicity in the friendship. But if you remain tight-lipped about the issues at hand, you can rest assure that they will never be resolved. They won't go away just because you wish them away.

The Difference

She needs to know what the qualities of a healthy friendship are, as well as those of an unhealthy/toxic one. She really may not know the difference! So share information about both. Refer her to relevant sources or provide her with such. She may be reluctant and unwilling to learn. And if that is the case, there's a fairly good chance that she doesn't care about the quality of the friendship or the way she treats you.

Your Role

Let your friend know how you have contributed to the toxicity of the friendship. You may have only contributed by perpetuating your friend's negative behaviors. If so, take responsibility for your role but don't let the perpetrator try to put the full blame in your hands and make you feel guilty.

The Specifics

Point out instances of toxic behavior when they occur. Again, she may not be aware of them, so you must tell her. Let the perpetrator know the very moment that a toxic, unfriendly, or unhealthy behavior occurs. Use *"I"* statements rather than *"You"* statements, even though she may have violated you in one way or another. Remember, it's about you and how you feel, not her. She may disagree with you and your perception of her negative behaviors and the impact they have on your relationship with her, so prepare yourself.

Ways to Communicate

Face to Face

- **Advantages:** You can get a sense of whether or not she is listening to you or ignoring you, and you can use your body language to help yourself relay the message.

- **Disadvantages:** She may interrupt you or try to silence you by making you feel guilty or making other negative comments in response to your truths. The chances of a physical confrontation also increase.

Telephone

- **Advantages:** She may interrupt you or try to silence you by making you feel guilty or making other negative comments, but you don't have to see her face or sit through her tell-all body language such as frowns, stares, eyes rolling, etc. And if the conversation gets too heated, you can simply hang up the phone.
- **Disadvantages:** She may hang up the phone before you have an opportunity to finish what you have to say. You can't see her body language, which might help you understand any verbal responses made to you.

Voice Mail

- **Advantages:** You can say what you have to say, and then hang up the phone. You don't have to engage in unfriendly conversation. And she'll also have a tape of your message to be used again, if need be. In other words, you don't have to repeat yourself; she can just replay the message if she doesn't *get it* the first time.
- **Disadvantages:** Your friend doesn't have a chance to respond, but she does have a taped message that can be used against you under certain circumstances. If you choose this method, speak in a calm manner and avoid swearing or using inappropriate language. Whatever message you leave, make sure it's one that you would allow the world to hear.

Letter, Email, or Text Message

- **Advantages:** You can say what you want without interruption and it will be in writing. Be sure to maintain the original message. Also, you can send this message again and again, if need be.

- **Disadvantages:** Your toxic friend will have a concrete reminder, but she'll also have something that could be used against you under certain circumstances. Just as with a voice mail, be careful about what you say and how you say it. Use lots of "I" statements and avoid swearing or using inappropriate language. Keep in mind that the information you put in writing can be forwarded very easily to others; so again, only write things that you would not mind the world reading!

Third Party Messenger (Another friend, relative, or co-worker)

- **Advantages:** This is a good way to avoid a verbal or physical confrontation with the perpetrator, especially if you're afraid of her or if a direct conversation between the two of you simply causes too much stress for you.
- **Disadvantages:** May cause conflict between your friend and the messenger, or the messenger may not deliver the message correctly by leaving out important details. This method may also be viewed as a cop-out, but who cares as long as the perpetrator understands the true intent of the message.

Mediator

- **Advantages:** The mediator could help ward off any verbal or physical confrontations between you and your toxic friend. In addition, the mediator could serve as a witness to behaviors that you might be unaware of in the midst of the conversation, especially if it's a heated one. She can also calm each of you down if tempers flare too high. She may have skills and training in conflict resolution or mediation in general. It could be a clergy person, counselor, administrator, etc. It could also be a mutual friend, but that could be an unfair situation for her to be in.
- **Disadvantages:** The mediator might show bias to either you or the perpetrator. Choosing a mediator could be difficult. She may not have the skills needed to deal with conflict resolution.

Greeting Card

- **Advantages:** Your message could be clearly stated, depending on the card you choose, but always add your own personal message. When using a blank greeting card, you can write your message inside the card. Greeting cards can be mailed, sent electronically, or handed directly to the perpetrator, if possible.
- **Disadvantage:** This method provides something concrete for your friend to read over and over again, but leaves you without any evidence that you communicated your concerns. Be sure to make a copy of the personal message you added to the card.

Alternative Methods of Communicating

Advances in technology have afforded us with various alternative methods of communication. However, like with the old-fashioned methods, things such as *farewell videos, DVDs, webcam messages,* or postings on *social media websites* should be used with great caution because they can have devastating effects on you if used improperly or sent to a deranged perpetrator.

In some instances, it will be appropriate to use one of the alternative methods; yet, in many cases, it will not be wise. Just as with letters, text messages, and emails, these things can also be shared with the masses. So before sending out a farewell message by video or posting on one of the social media sites, be sure it is something that you would not mind seeing splattered over the internet if your toxic friend should get pissed off and post it without your permission.

Important Note: If you choose a method that doesn't require direct contact with the perpetrator, that's OK. Do not consider it a cop-out because you didn't choose a method that fits her needs or boosts her ego any more than necessary. After all, the purpose of telling her the truth is so you can begin your own personal healing and take care of yourself. If she or anyone else criticizes you about the way you choose to convey your message, remember that it's their issue – not yours.

You may have to use a combination of methods or repeat the same method before you make your point. If your friend is in denial about her behaviors or clueless as to how you're feeling, she may never comprehend what you're trying to convey to her. Telling the perpetrator the truth offers no guarantee that she will change her toxic behaviors, but at least you can have peace of mind knowing that you let her know about them.

Change Your Behavior

The chances of the perpetrator changing her behaviors are pretty slim; therefore, you must change yours. The most important change you can make is learning to say "No" without second thoughts or guilt feelings. You must also change the way you react and respond to her ill-treatment of you. You may have to kill her with kindness or hurt her with truth and honesty. Either way, the goal is to free yourself from the toxicity and restore your own well-being. You will have to do so by any means possible and/or necessary.

Take a Look in the Mirror

When dealing with a toxic friendship, one must stop and ask this question: *"What have I done to contribute to the toxicity?"* You may not feel that you're responsible for any of it. But the truth is that you are, although the level of responsibility varies from person to person. You may not have pulled the trigger or loaded the gun, but you may have provided the ammunition by rationalizing, accepting, justifying, or even ignoring the perpetrator's ill-treatment of you. It's true that you cannot change her behavior but you can manipulate the outcome of its negative effects on you by monitoring your own words, actions, and reactions. Watch what you say, when you say it, and how you say it.

Put Yourself First and Foremost

Shift the focus from the perpetrator onto yourself. Oftentimes, victims spend an enormous amount of time and energy caring for the needs and concerns of their toxic friends while neglecting their own. And as selfish as it may seem, one must develop a *"me, myself, and I"* attitude, otherwise the perpetrator will continue to take advantage and treat the victim (you) in an unfriendly manner.

Consider Ending the Friendship

Consider terminating the friendship before it gets any worse than it already is. If you don't feel the friendship is worth keeping, free yourself. It may not be easy but it might be in your best interest to do so. The perpetrator's negative behavior could land you in a world of trouble and cause a lot of continued and unnecessary stress, strain, and anxiety in your life. Even though you may put forth your best efforts, you won't be able to change her behavior.

How Others Handled It

The way you chose to deal with your toxic friend depends on your individual circumstances. Some may have to be kept at arms length, while others may only need to have a clarification of what boundaries she is not to cross. Still, others may have to be removed from your life altogether. Here's how real victims dealt/coped with their toxic friends …

Survey Question: Briefly explain how you currently or previously dealt with your friend's toxic behavior(s).

Responses:

> *At the present time, we don't really talk or see each other, and it has been this way over the past year.*

> *I've given our friendship lots of space. Where we used to talk on the phone daily, I maybe talk to her on the phone once a month.*

At first I soft-pedaled her histrionics and ignored her ill-behavior, rationalizing everything that was said and done, hoping that with my example of calm and reason she would change. Eventually I faded her out of my life. It was very difficult.

I just left her alone and got busy. I was not available to her anymore.

Stopped telling her stuff.

I would stay away from her so that we didn't have to argue.

I have made up my mind that I will no longer allow this person to get under my skin, stopped allowing myself to loan out my money, and only deal with this person when I want to be bothered.

I told her that I needed air and that I was not the type of person that was constantly underneath friends. Then I moved away without giving her my new address or phone.

I confronted her about how she treated me and how I felt in the friendship.

I'll usually avoid answering her calls, etc., for a few weeks. It sounds odd but that's the nature of our friendship. We only hang out together twice a month or so.

I told her I was not able to meet her expectations, and that her comments reminded me of other situations I'd been in that were similar, and I didn't feel safe.

While these victims took some type of action towards resolving their toxic friendships, many others didn't for one reason or another.

The following are examples of how some victims chose to unsuccessfully deal with their toxic friends:

I am not dealing.

I try not to say anything to hurt anyone's feelings.

Didn't say much and cried a lot.

I would give in every time; I'd always apologize, even if I wasn't in the wrong.

Overlooked or made excuses for the behavior.

I just try to shrug it off in public, but in private I'm an emotional mess.

I just go with the flow.

I usually gave her the benefit of the doubt ... there was probably a good reason for her behaviors.

Many times, the way some victims choose to deal with their toxic friendships often fuels the toxicity. Their efforts often give the perpetrator even more incentive to maintain her toxic behavior. Some of their methods are just Band-Aids or temporary solutions to an ongoing problem.

Self-Evaluation

If you are currently trapped in a toxic friendship, think about what steps you have taken thus far to resolve the problems you are having ...

List them in the space below.

_____

_____

_____

_____

_____

If you couldn't think of anything that you may have done, here's one for you ...

By taking the time to read this book, you have taken a big step in educating yourself about toxic friendships, and education is a key component to overcoming and conquering the ills of an unhealthy friendship.

If you have tried some things that didn't work, try some new ones. But whatever you do, don't let a toxic friendship take away the best of you.

ELIMINATING TOXIC FRIENDS FROM YOUR LIFE

Reality *Check*

Some toxic friendships may be worth saving, while most are probably not ... it's all personal.

Best Friends Forever ... Dispel the Myth

Friendship is like a marriage in that it is a relationship that requires the commitment of two people. Sometimes the bond between two best friends is synonymous and just as important as the bond between a husband and a wife. And just like a marriage, friendships can have issues and trouble, and therefore need to end. A closely bonded friendship often reaps some of the benefits similar to those of a marriage. And we often try to maintain these unhealthy friendships for many of the same reasons we maintain unhealthy marriages because in many cases a best friend can be considered a second significant other.

Unfortunately, one mistake that many victims make is to believe that their long-term friendships will last forever and that these relationships cannot become toxic over time. Keep in mind that the perpetrator can be someone you have only known for a short time, someone you grew up with, or someone you have known for many years. The length of time of a friendship is not a prerequisite to being BFF. Long-term friendships *can* become toxic over time. And even though the impact of a toxic friendship can lead to mental stress and strain, physical ailments, loss of self-esteem and one's identify, financial and relationship issues, etc., people tend to hold onto these unhealthy friendships anyway.

Why do we hold on for so long? Why can't we just let go of our toxic friendships? The reasons are varied but nevertheless produce the same outcome ...

Toxic Strongholds

Victims remain trapped in toxic friendships for various reasons. But many remained trapped because of the *Toxic Strongholds* that seem to almost justify their reasons for not ending an unhealthy relationship. They keep them emotionally trapped in toxicity to the point where they feel like they cannot live their life without their toxic friend. Even though the toxic friendship brings much sorrow and pain, at times; it's also a place of comfort and momentary refuge from one's problems, issues, and personal drama.

In some cases, victims have a strong need to feel needed. And their toxic friend is the only one capable of fulfilling that need ... or so they think. The unhappiness they feel as a result of the toxic friendship generally takes a backseat as they continue to suffer, usually in silence. And for many, Toxic Strongholds overshadow the reality of the friendship altogether, making the victim a perpetual prisoner of toxicity.

Below is an overview of the various types of Toxic Strongholds that can plague an unhealthy friendship. Keep in mind that as valid as they may all seem, these are simply excuses for not wanting to find an effective means of dealing with a toxic friend.

History

Victims who have been involved with a toxic friend for a long length of time will use this as an excuse to remain in a toxic friendship. As they contemplate ending it, they often get sidetracked by the constant mental reminders that they have known the perpetrator for such a long time and they have done so many things together. They don't want to throw away that history by ending the friendship. They would rather continue to take whatever their toxic friend dishes out, whether it's good or bad.

Kinship

Some victims are best friends with a relative by blood or marriage. Either way, the kinship creates an obstacle for some because they don't want to hurt their family member by revealing the truth about the dissatisfaction and unhappiness they feel with the relationship. So the victims pretend as if nothing is wrong in an effort to keep peace within the family.

Familiarity

Sometimes victims form a very close bond and a high level of intimacy with their friend. When that happens, they unconsciously or consciously refer to her as their sister or cousin. When they think about the possibility of ending a friendship with them, it's almost as if they would be losing a family member. And it's not always easy to remove a family member from your life.

Fear

Sometimes fear causes victims to feel anxious and worried about what life might be like without their toxic friend. The fear can brainwash them and cause them to become emotionally paralyzed. They aren't able to think rationally and understand that they can have a good life without their toxic friend being a part of it. Toxic friends sometimes become crutches, and many people feel that if they end a close toxic friendship, they will be left friendless.

Rejection

Although we know our toxic friendships are unhealthy for us and we know we need to end them, we sometimes don't. Once we tell a toxic friend that we need to end the friendship, we risk the chance of getting a backlash of rejection. But sometimes we need to go through that painful rejection process because it can make the transition from a toxic friendship a bit easier.

Wishful Thinking

The false hopes and promises that we harbor keep us trapped in toxicity. We want our most treasured friendships to last forever, but the reality is that sometimes they don't. If there is a glimmer of hope that the friendship could get better, we hold on to it for dear life. When we listen to the perpetrators apologize for mistreating us and promising that they won't do it again, we can't help but give the friendship just *one* more try. This type of thinking works for a little while until we get a reality check. That's when we realize that it's not going to get any better. The perpetrator is never going to change, and if we don't make some changes in the way we deal with her or end the friendship altogether, the bad things will only get worse.

Shame

Some victims are ashamed and embarrassed about having to admit the demise of their close friendship. Having to admit the fact that there is trouble in friendship paradise is like an admission of failure for some victims. They struggle with what others will say or think about them, if they end the friendship. Facing their public with news that they are ending a once treasured; but now toxic friendship, is not an option for some victims. They would rather continue the friendship as if nothing is wrong.

Confusion

With all the mixed messages that toxic friends give us, we sometimes don't know what to do. So we love them one day and hate them the next. They'll do a positive thing to overshadow the negative thing they did to us days ago, which only perpetuates the *Cycle of Toxicity*. Their unpredictable behavior and actions cause emotional confusion for us as we try to sift through the good times and the bad times. We try to rationalize their behavior and actions, as well as our own. We began to think that we are the crazy ones.

Personal Ignorance

Many people want to end their toxic friendships but they often say they don't know how. But if ending the toxic friendship is your ultimate goal, you will find a way. You may have to try several times, as well as different methods, but you must keep on trying until you free yourself. More than likely, your toxic friend won't help you end it, so you have to be vigilant in your efforts. Don't be ashamed to seek help and/or advice or assistance from others. You may not realize it, but sometimes it's necessary to have someone help you to relay the message to the perpetrator. You may have to solicit the support of someone like a sister, cousin, mutual friend, parent, etc., to reiterate your desire to end the friendship with your toxic friend if she isn't taking *you* seriously.

Guilt

Some victims send themselves on extreme guilt trips when they start thinking about ending their toxic friendships. The guilt becomes so powerful that they find themselves forever trapped in toxicity. They feel guilty because the perpetrator depends on them for one thing or another, and if they end the friendship, they worry about how their friend will survive without them.

Culpability

Sometimes you may think that you're going crazy while dealing with your toxic friend. Some perpetrators are good at making you feel that way. They somehow place the blame for all the negative stuff that happens in their life and in the friendship, *on you*. They make you feel like you have really done something wrong, so that they can justify their own unhealthy behavior. It's much easier for the perpetrator to say, *"It's your fault"* because you are the one speaking out against the way the friendship is going. And hearing that from her over and over again will eventually cause you to start questioning and blaming yourself.

Loneliness

The need and desire for companionship keeps many victims trapped in toxic friendships. For some, a toxic friend is better than having no friend at all. So many people would rather deal with the ill treatment of the perpetrator rather than the emptiness that they would feel if they had no friend at all. A toxic friendship for a lonely person is a place of refuge, a place where they can cower down into emotional safety. They often feel that the perpetrator is only one who really understands them.

Low Self-Esteem

Victims with low self-esteem often find themselves trapped in toxic friendships because they simply don't think they deserve to have a better-quality friendship. They often see themselves as failures, and believe they're not worthy of anything good. So why should friendships be any different? They hold onto toxic friendships as a means of validation and confirmation that somebody *likes* them and *wants* to be their friend, even though the perpetrator treats them badly.

Obligation

Sometimes we remain in toxic friendships out of loyalty, even when the perpetrator has mistreated us and abused the friendship. She may be the friend of your spouse, the mother of your child's best friend, a neighbor, co-worker, etc. Because of certain relationships and/or *connections,* we somehow feel obligated to keep the friendship going so other folks won't turn against us. Other victims may feel obligated because of a favor or gesture done by the perpetrator, and remaining in the friendship is a way of paying back the perpetrator.

Regret

Regret is a stronghold for some because they're concerned about the possibility of needing the perpetrator in the future for one thing or another. But if the friendship is ended for valid reasons, such as toxicity, there should be no need for regret. If you end the friendship for frivolous reasons; then perhaps you will experience some regret at a later time. That is why it's very important to validate your reasons for ending the friendship.

Mercy

The right thing to do is to forgive those who do us wrong. It's imperative that we do just that for our own healing to begin to take place. Unfortunately, for many victims, this creates a problem because of the fragility of their own state of mind when they are involved with an unhealthy friendship. It's not unusual for them to misinterpret their own forgiveness and compassion as signs of weakness or an invitation to continue doing business as usual, thus rendering the perpetrator the upper hand to continue her toxic behaviors.

Pity

Sometimes victims feel so sorry for their toxic friends for one reason or another and they want to help them. After all, that's what friends are for, right? We feel that if we leave them, they will be friendless – not realizing that some of them need to be left temporarily friendless until they get their acts together! If we leave them, know that they will quickly find someone else to infect with their toxicity. They are pros at what they do. If you feel the need to walk away from a toxic friendship, do it! The perpetrator will be just fine.

These are just some of the toxic strongholds or reasons why people remain in toxic friendships. If you're holding on to a toxic friendship for any of these reasons, keep this in mind: the longer you give in to one or more of these toxic strongholds (as well as any others), the longer you will remain trapped in toxicity.

As you can see, the reasons for holding on to a toxic friendship are as varied as the types of toxic friends. Everyone has their reasons and justifications. During my research, I discovered that although there was a wide variety of reasons why people held on to their toxic friendships, the most common reason appears to be based on the level of intimacy among the friends as well as the length of time of the friendship.

A common response was *"We've been friends forever!"*

Survey Questions & Answers

Survey Question: When you realized your friendship was toxic/ unhealthy, did you remain in it?

Response: More than 95% of the over 2800 respondents answered *"Yes"* to this question.

Survey Question: If yes (to the previous question), what are or were your reasons for holding on to the friendship?

Responses:

I had made promises. The person relied on me so heavily, I was afraid she wouldn't survive without me. It took me a year to break it off, and another year to stop feeling guilty.

I couldn't find an adequate reason to end the friendship – I didn't know HOW to end it even though I was very unhappy.

We had built up a relationship that I wanted to keep after having invested so much time and energy and I was also very lonely.

She didn't mean what she said! She was "stressed" and unhappy. I was the only person who really understood her. We had a lot in common, same occupation and shared the same hobby. I wanted to avoid confronting her as she'd get very angry or very sad.

I like her a lot, our friendship means a lot to me and we work together. I don't want to create tension. We also share some friends and she can get really vengeful and nasty when things go sour so I just try to keep the peace.

I was lonely and thought she was the only person in my life (but now I know that I made it that way). When I first met her, she was suicidal; I felt a strong need to be there for her.

I felt bad for her. Everyone gave up on her. She had a hard life and is still having it hard. I didn't want to give up because I would have felt like I failed God.

Because we have been friends for so long and I didn't realize she was such a bitch until the past two years.

I felt sorry for her and thought it was only a "phase." I thought she would change and I believed her every time she would tell me she was sorry.

At first I just chalked it up to believing, "That's just the way she is," and accepted her for who she was. She has no support group, she had lost her dog and husband in less than a year, and she has no children. I didn't want to abandon her at a time when she needed support.

I hoped that she was different with me than other people and that my friendship would maybe change her.

Our children were friends and we had mutual friends.

She wasn't always like this. She was a great, true friend then she caved into her addictions. I thought she'd get back on track but she never did, so I left.

She knows everything about me, including deep secrets and weaknesses that can ruin my life. I told her some things about myself which I hadn't told anyone else and felt she had a hold on me.

I'm by myself in a city where I don't know anyone else. I guess I'm afraid I won't make another group of friends.

I thought she might change her ways. I thought I could make her have some sense every now and then.

It's too much hassle to end the friendship fully.

We've been friends for a long time. We have a lot of history and I always felt that because of the drama, I needed to be there to help her.

I felt sorry for her. She was having a hard time. I didn't want to lose a friendship. I thought she would grow out of her behavior.

I tried to give her several chances and I didn't want to hurt her. I knew she had suffered rejection in the past and I didn't want to add to this. She promised to go to counseling.

I thought she was just going through a temporary phase in her life and the fact was that I didn't want to be judgmental.

I felt sorry for her because she had no one in the whole world. Even her brothers didn't speak to her.

I have true friendship feelings for her almost sister-like and don't want to let go. I decided to keep things inside whenever she upset me. Then I'd just let it go and pretend like nothing happened just so she wouldn't suspect that I was mad or hurt, even when I was.

Our families are very close and there's the longevity of the friendship. We have several very close mutual friends.

I am too afraid to stand up to her and afraid of her messing up my other friendships, and making me the scapegoat.

I always thought the problem was me because I didn't understand what was happening.

I felt I was strong enough to stick it out and try to help her become a better person.

I stayed in the friendship because I thought she would change but I know now that it's not going to happen.

I really treasured our friendship and thought it would be a failure to end it. I've never flat out ended a friendship before.

She's my sister-in-law. She had a terrible past and no other strong female relationships in her life. I thought she needed me and I felt trapped in the friendship.

I thought I was the problem and that I was messed up somehow or damaged and that she was the wonderful, devoted friend. She tries to convince me of that all the time.

We're in business together and we've been friends for so long and ending the friendship would hurt too much.

As you can see, the reasons for holding onto a toxic friendship vary from person to person. Do any of them sound familiar to you?

○ Yes
○ No

Letting Go of the Toxicity

Toxic friendships, no matter how unsatisfying; have a tendency of making the victim feel like they are caught between a rock and a hard place. Victims love their toxic friends and despise them at the same time. Nevertheless, despite the ill-treatment, misuse, and abuse in the friendship; victims tend to continue spending time with the perpetrators anyway.

You are the perpetrator's *"best friend"* or *"best fool"* as long as you continue to comply with her requests of your time, energy, money, or whatever else she can muster out of you.

Even still, if a toxic friendship does come to an end, the break-up is most often initiated by the victim rather than the perpetrator as indicated on the graph on the next page.

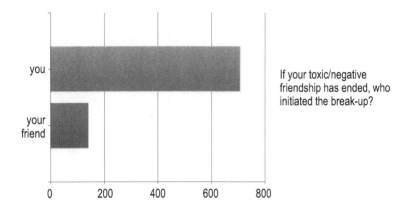

If your toxic/negative friendship has ended, who initiated the break-up?

Methods for Ending a Toxic Friendship

Although there are many ways to eliminate a toxic friend from your life, only sane and sensible ways will be discussed here. You must evaluate your own friendship and determine which way is best for you, based on the circumstances of your toxic friendship. What might work for one toxic friendship may not work for another.

The method you choose for ending your toxic friendship will certainly depend on many factors, such as the intimacy level, the extent of the bond between you and your toxic friend, the length of time you've known your friend, as well as other individual factors. If you're casual friends with someone, it may be easier to end the friendship than it is with someone really close to you emotionally.

In general, there are three main ways you can break off a friendship with a toxic friend.

- Cold Turkey
- Weaning
- Let It Fade Away

Cold Turkey

Using the Cold Turkey method of ending your toxic friendship is by far the most difficult way to end it if you have a strong emotional bond with your friend. This method involves ending the friendship abruptly. It means cutting your toxic friend out of your life all at once, no questions asked and no reasons discussed. It's not necessarily an easy way to end a toxic friendship, but it can be an effective and quick way to put a stop to it and move on with your life. But you must have a strong will to want to leave it behind and end it once and for all. And keep in mind that it's not always easy to overcome the emotional impacts of losing a close friendship.

On the other hand, if you don't have an emotional bond with your friend or if the connection has been shattered due to the toxicity in the friendship, this method will no doubt be faster and easier for you. In most cases, you can just state your intentions to the perpetrator and then move on with your life.

Either way, in order to be fair to yourself and to the perpetrator as well, be sure to communicate your intentions. If you care about the perpetrator on some level and she cares about you, one of the worse things you can do is just walk away from the friendship without saying a word. Even if you don't think your friend deserves a final word from you, give it to her anyway. It will give you peace of mind and decrease the chances of you feeling any guilt or regret later on.

If you choose the Cold Turkey method for ending your toxic friendship, be sure to stick to your guns. If the perpetrator is very manipulative, she may be able to get you to change your decision. She might tell you that she wants to work on the friendship, that she is willing to change her behavior, or that she is sorry and won't do *it* (whatever it may be) again. She will try her best to push your sympathy buttons.

Show a little compassion, even if you are really angry with the perpetrator. Caring about the perpetrator and having concern for her is normal and won't necessarily decrease immediately after you end the friendship. It may take days, weeks, months, or even years for it to lessen. In fact, the care and concern for your friend may never end, but that doesn't mean you should have any guilt whatsoever about your decision to walk away from your toxic friendship nor should it keep you trapped in it. Don't beat yourself down because you still care about your toxic friend!

Weaning

Just like mothers wean their babies off the bottle or breast, adults have to sometimes wean themselves from things they like or have been accustomed to having. Such things, if held on to for too long, will become bad habits in their lives - such as maintaining toxic friendships.

Weaning oneself from a valued friendship is sometimes difficult to do because making the transition from being best friends to acquaintances will not occur overnight. It is indeed *a process.* So if you decide to use this method, it will be wise to inform your toxic friend of your intentions. She may or may not stick around to see it through to the end.

However, if she does stick around and refuses to accept the reality, just prepare yourself for a possible onslaught of negative feelings, emotions, accusations, responses, and reactions from her. She may become critical and accuse you of not caring about her, not being fair, making her feel bad on purpose, etc.

She may respond to the weaning process by calling you nasty names, yelling at you, and saying bad things about you. She may also try to make you feel guilty by using manipulative statements such as: *"Look at all the stuff I've done for you"* or *"You act as if I don't even exist."* And it may very well be your intent to act as if she doesn't exist, if that is what it takes to eliminate her from your life. Don't allow her to influence your behaviors or decisions about how you choose to wean her from your life.

You will have to become a vigilant fighter in your emotional battle and make a vow to yourself to be victorious, even if it takes multiple tries. If your goal is to wean yourself from your toxic friendship, you must not fall prey to the setbacks and road blocks that she will undoubtedly throw your way.

Tips for Weaning

Clean House

Be sure to take care of any and all unfinished business with the perpetrator. Return or retrieve all necessary items, complete unfinished partner projects, pay owed debts, etc.

Communicate Your Intentions

Let her know of your intentions to end the friendship with her and be done with it. There's no need for an elaborate verbal battle about it.

Learn to Say "No" and Make It Stick

Start saying "NO" to the perpetrator and refusing or denying her requests for your time, energy, resources, or whatever; even if you really don't want to do so. "NO" is a small but powerful word that speaks volumes if you use it often and consistently.

Change the Way You Communicate

- Decrease the methods you use to communicate with your friend and decide on just one (e.g. cell, text, email, etc.) for your weaning period. Cut loose of all the others. Let her know which form of communication you will accept from her; then ignore all attempts by any other methods.
- Let the perpetrator initiate any future communications with you, then you can decide when to respond and how often (but only by the means you selected as your mode of communicating with her).

- When communicating with your toxic friend, make the conversations short but sweet and as impersonal as possible; remember you're trying to wean yourself from this friendship.
- When you're ready, decrease the number of times she is allowed to communicate with you. For instance, if your method of communication with her is via email and she emails you five times per day and you respond to each one, you will have to discipline yourself to start decreasing the number of emails you respond to and eventually stop responding altogether. This holds true for all forms of communication, regardless of which one you selected to use during the weaning phase.

Stay Away From Her

- Decrease the amount of time you spend with the perpetrator; don't visit her home or allow her to visit yours unless absolutely necessary.
- Once you decide to wean yourself, don't plan any future activities with the perpetrator.
- If you have previously planned activities that you have not done yet, find a way to get out of doing it with that person. If you can't get out of it, then put on a happy face, adopt a positive attitude, and do the activity. But let her know that it is not business as usual and that you are not trying to remain friends with her. She needs to know this without any doubt whatsoever; that the only reason you are doing the activity is because it was already planned and there was no way out. However, if there is a way out, then take it!

Maintain Your Professionalism

- If you work with your friend, keep in mind that it's important to remain professional; the whole office doesn't have to know your business. You can say *"Hello"* and *"Good-bye"* to each other just like everyone else.

- If possible, eliminate your contact with the perpetrator. Don't have breaks or lunch with her; don't volunteer to work on projects with her. If you work in close proximity, perhaps your boss or supervisor can change your work location.
- Don't discuss your friend with others, but it would be wise to let co-workers know that you have broken off the friendship so that they won't talk to you about her and vice versa. If you prefer, you can try to keep the break-up a secret; however, if the two of you were close and everyone in the office knew that, it might be better to get the news out in the open before the rumors start to fly.

Seek Emotional Support

- Breaking up with a close friend can be very painful. In fact, it hurts like hell. Talk to your other friends and your family about what's going on and how you feel. You don't have to say negative things about your friend; instead use "I" phrases, such as *"I feel so used and betrayed"* or *"I knew something just wasn't right with the friendship." "I don't understand how she could treat me this way."*
- Whatever you do, even though the reason for the break-up could be mostly due to your friend's behavior, try not to play the blame game.

Important Note about Weaning

If you do decide to wean yourself, don't listen to people who tell you to *"get over it"* when you start feeling sad or blue because you miss the companionship of your toxic friend. Those may be people who have never had a closely bonded friendship and obviously do not realize that you don't just *"get over it."* It takes time. You'll get over it or at the very least feel a sense of satisfaction at some point. Just keep in mind that during the weaning process, you have to let time heal your wounds. You may find yourself grieving the loss of the toxic friendship for a very long time and that's OK.

Let It Fade Away

Sometimes you may not have to consciously do either of the above in order to eliminate a toxic friend from your life. The friendship may simply fade away. This may be due to lifestyle changes, interests, finances, relocation, new friendships, other relationships, career expectations, family responsibilities, or whatever.

Things that occur in your life may unintentionally take the focus off of your toxic friendship and the stress of it all. And as a result, you shift your energy to focus on more important things. Thus you begin to spend less time and energy dealing with your toxic friend, which ultimately leads to separation, distance, and a lack of interest in maintaining the friendship.

Things to Consider When Ending a Toxic Friendship

Don't Give Up

Many victims don't realize that ending a toxic friendship may take some time, as well as several unsuccessful attempts at walking away and staying away. As a result, they beat themselves up if they end the friendship then retreat back to it repeatedly. This usually occurs after their toxic friend apologizes and vows to never repeat the negative behavior(s) again, thus repeating the *Cycle of Toxicity*. It's not unusual to make several unsuccessful attempts at ending a toxic friendship, but that's OK. If emotional freedom and rediscovery of self is your ultimate goal, you must be vigilant in your efforts. If at first, you don't succeed … keep on trying!

Don't Expect a Quick Emotional Disconnection

No matter how much disappointment your toxic friendship has caused, the emotional bond and connection that you have with her is not going to diminish overnight. We often allow our emotions to distort our common sense, which can become nonsense as we try to decipher the confusion that plagues our minds. One minute our friend is the perfect friend and the next she's the epitome of a devil in disguise, and that's enough confusion in and of itself. Unfortunately, the emotional disconnect that we seek won't be easy so just be patient with yourself. It's going to take some time.

Don't Hold Your Breath Waiting For Change

It's easy for victims to accept their toxic friend back into their lives after they have attempted to end the friendship. This is because they want to believe that their toxic friend can change her behavior. And she can, but it has to be because she wants to and not as a condition for you to allow her back into your life.

Below is what twenty-seven-year-old Corrine concluded about her friend Nancy *changing* her toxic behaviors:

> *After ten years, I realized that no matter what I did she was not going to change the way she treated me. I had humiliated myself for so long and I was tired of it. I was tired of being there for someone who refused to be there for me. According to her, she allowed me to be around her and that should have been good enough.*

Victims must realize that change doesn't occur overnight and sometimes it never happens. If you decide to walk away from the perpetrator today, then she calls you up two days later and says, *"Hey I've changed and I promise I won't ever repeat the toxic behavior(s) again,"* you might want to rethink your decision about rekindling the relationship and allowing her back into your life so quickly. Your friend needs quantitative time to change and a few days just doesn't cut it. Sometimes not even a couple of months will change things, as Jen wrote about her toxic friendship of two years:

> *I tried at least five times to end this friendship but each time she apologized and/or made me feel guilty. She made me believe I*

was the one in the wrong so that I would apologize and still be her friend. She also told me how much she loves me no matter what. But this time, I told her I had finally had enough when she did something totally unforgivable. Two months later she called and apologized, but her behaviors have not changed. She's still doing the same old stuff to me so I've decided to end all communication with her. She has yet to try to contact me, so we will see what happens. I haven't visited her in several months and I don't plan on ever doing so again.

Not only does your toxic friend need time to change her behavior(s), so do you. You need to change the way you react and respond to her as well. That's generally how you begin the process of eliminating her from your life, physically as well as emotionally.

Ending a toxic friendship is like ending any other relationship; the emotional disconnect will not happen overnight, even if you use the cold turkey method. This is a process, and it can be a very difficult one for those who have a long history or a deep emotional bond with their toxic friend. Once you break off the physical relationship with the perpetrator, you will have to deal with the emotional and mental aspects of the break-up as well. And this is often the most difficult part. The greater the level of intimacy, the harder it is to end a toxic friendship. So don't beat yourself down if you don't have the will power to stay away from the perpetrator after you have walked away and tried to end the friendship for the very first or even the second time. It may take multiple tries before you achieve your desired outcome – which is to successfully remove the perpetrator from your life.

Self-Evaluation

Think about your toxic friendship …

Have you *ever* tried to end it and failed to do so?

○ Yes
○ No

If yes, list the reasons why your attempts may have failed in the past.

_____

_____

_____

_____

_____

If you have *never* tried to end your toxic friendship, what are you waiting for? List your excuses in the space below.

_____

_____

_____

_____

_____

Now take some time to think about and answer these simple questions …*Why am I holding on? What are my toxic strongholds or reasons for remaining in this unhealthy friendship? Write your answers below.*

_____

_____

_____

_____

_____

Do any of your reasons make sense?

○ Yes
○ No

If not, then ask yourself this question ...*What am I going to do about it?*

After giving this question some serious consideration, write your thoughts in the space below.

DEALING WITH THE AFTERMATH
OF A TOXIC FRIENDSHIP

Reality *Check*

If you have successfully ended your toxic friendship, the perpetrator can now appropriately be referred to as your former toxic friend or FTF ... remember that!

The Friendship Is Over ... Now What?

At this point, you're probably asking yourself a few questions, "*What do I do now?*" "*I got rid on my toxic friend but why do I feel so sad and lonely?*" *What will I do without her?* "*We did everything together!*" That's probably true but now it's time to put the past behind you and move on. This may be difficult but it's what you have to do in order to regain your freedom and independence from toxicity and to rediscover yourself. And if you think that breaking up with your friend was the most difficult journey on your road to freedom, think again. Your true battle has just begun, especially if your FTF refused to accept your decision to walk away from the friendship. Whatever you do, don't take this battle for granted; it is one of the most important battles you'll encounter because it is one that will lead you down the path of self-rediscovery without your toxic friend. That is your ultimate goal, right?

Whatever your friend took away from you (or you consciously or unconsciously gave to her), it's time to recoup *some* of your losses. Unfortunately, some things will be lost forever and are irreparable. But there is a light at the end of the tunnel as you begin the journey of living your life without your FTF.

Here are a few suggestions for making your journey a bit smoother.

Forgive Your FTF

Although each toxic friendship is unique, there are some general things you can do to aid in your recovery – including forgiving your FTF. It's important to forgive her for whatever you feel she has done to you. Forgiveness is necessary in order for you to heal; however, no one can tell you when and how to forgive. It must be done when you are ready and by whichever means you choose to relay the forgiveness.

Communicating Your Forgiveness

Verbally

This form of communication should only be used if you ended your toxic friendship but *have continued to communicate infrequently* with your FTF on some level. You can call her on the phone or tell her face to face. You can also leave a voice message if you prefer not to have an actual conversation with her.

- **Advantages:** Verbally declaring your forgiveness may make you feel good inside and feel less guilty about ending the friendship.
- **Disadvantages:** Your FTF may consider your verbal forgiveness as a sign of weakness and an indication that you want to rekindle a friendship with her. It could also draw you back into increased communication with her, as you might find yourself trying to prove your forgiveness.

Nonverbally

This form of communication should only be used if you feel you are not emotionally strong enough to communicate verbally with your FTF.

- **Advantages:** You can forgive your FTF via email, text message, greeting card, or any other form of nonverbal communication without having a verbal conversation with her.
- **Disadvantages:** You may not find peace knowing that you didn't communicate your forgiveness verbally.

Technologically

Technology affords us many opportunities to relay messages to others. In addition to text messages and emails, you can also post your forgiveness on social networking sites, personal blogs, video web sharing sites, etc.

- **Advantages:** You can forgive your FTF without ever having to *see* her face or *hear* her voice.
- **Disadvantages:** Most likely your postings will not be private, any and everyone may have access to your message of forgiveness.

Alternative Method of Forgiving

In Your Heart

If you don't feel comfortable communicating your forgiveness either verbally or nonverbally, you can forgive your FTF in your heart.

- **Advantages:** You don't have to worry about communicating with your FTF or proving to her that she has been forgiven.
- **Disadvantages:** Your FTF may never know that you have forgiven her.

Whatever method you decide to use is entirely up you and should be based on your individual circumstances. Remember, you don't have to prove anything to anyone, especially your FTF.

Myths about Forgiving

- It means that you forget what has happened to you.
- It is a sign of weakness or defeat.
- It has to be repeated, duplicated, or proven to your FTF.
- It's an easy to thing to do.
- It happens quickly and/or overnight.
- It is not required for your own personal healing.

Identify Your Role

Identify the role you played in the demise of your former toxic friendship. Were you an enabler or just a passive victim? Take some time to evaluate yourself and your own behavior. Your friend may have been toxic indeed, but what about you? Ask yourself what you may have done to contribute to the toxicity. You may think you did nothing wrong, but it takes two people to *continue* an unhealthy relationship. Think about the way you may have responded or reacted to the perpetrators negative behavior towards you. Were you angry, did you lash out at her or did you seek any type of revenge? Knowing what your own faults were will help you prevent the same mistakes from occurring in future friendships.

Face the Facts

The friendship is over! Whether you or your FTF ended it, it's over and it is time to move on with your life. As stated previously, some friendships don't last forever. And the sooner you accept that fact, the sooner you will be able to start your new life without your FTF. It may be very emotionally painful in the beginning, but time will heal most, if not all, of your wounds.

Set Necessary Boundaries

Your FTF needs to know *what is* and *what is not* allowed within the realm of your disconnect from her. It is not wise to think that unspoken boundaries are sufficient enough to ward off the possible unwanted or negative behaviors and reactions of your FTF. Even though you may have made it perfectly clear that the friendship is over, sometimes the perpetrator just won't go away. So setting clear and concise boundaries is a necessary task.

The types of boundaries you set will depend greatly on your individual circumstances. Here are a few you may want to consider:

- Communication
- Aid and Assistance
- Personal
- Financial
- Physical
- Emotional
- Visitation

Important Note: These boundaries are not only for your FTF but for yourself as well.

Don't Make Excuses

It is what it is; you cannot change your FTF, make her treat you more kindly, make her behave as you wish, etc. If the friendship wasn't a right fit and you have chosen to move on, good for you. Coping with the loss of this friendship, no matter how toxic you found it to be, can be difficult if there was an emotional bond. But if the friendship was unhealthy and destructive in nature, the emotional bond you think you may have had could have just been an excuse for you to keep dwelling on the *maybes* or the *what-ifs* … *"Maybe I should have given her another chance"* … *"What-if I was too harsh on her"* … *"Maybe she was just having a bad day," "What-if I overreacted to her behavior"*, etc. Those *maybes* and *what-ifs* will keep you trapped between guilt and regret. And it's not worth it.

Emotional Limitations

As humans, our capacity to deal with negative emotions has a limit. And once we reach that limit, we must take action to reverse its negative impact on our lives or else we put our mental health and emotional well-being in jeopardy.

Unfortunately, many victims don't realize just how much those negative feelings and emotions were generated as a result of their association with their FTF, nor the extent of the impact on their everyday lives. Therefore, they don't consider their emotional well-being and mental health as being in disrepair, mainly because of the stigma attached to those who choose to do so. But if you aren't conscious of your emotional and mental instability or you deny it; during this tumultuous time in your life, you may suffer greatly. It is important that you familiarize yourself with the signs of emotional stress and strain so that you can find ways to combat it.

Signs of Emotional Stress and Strain

Here are just a few common signs of emotional stress and strain. This is not an inclusive list. You may have other signs that aren't listed here but that doesn't lessen their importance.

- Depression, sadness
- Isolation, wanting to be alone
- Constant anxiety, agitation, and irritation
- Constant fatigue, body aches, and pain
- Anger towards others for no reasons
- Extreme emotional sensitivity, crying
- Loss of interest in things you once enjoyed
- Trouble sleeping
- Eating disorders
- Substance abuse

Dealing with a toxic friend can drain your emotions and cause a lot of physical and emotional stress and strain. If not dealt with properly, this will no doubt take its toll on you. And when you are no longer able to deal with the emotional assaults, you may want to consider seeking some type of professional intervention in order to save yourself from falling into a deep state of depression. If you are already at that point, you may need professional counseling, guidance, or support to pull you out of your current state.

Survey Question & Answers

Survey Question: How does or did the toxic/negative friendship affect you emotionally?

Responses:

It's draining, and I'm cross with myself for my lack of honesty and the guts to at least say something to her.

I feel continuously frustrated, angry, upset, sad, and fearful.

It demoralized me and made me feel that I was worthless. It damaged my marriage and hurt my children. It wasn't worth it.

I became very depressed and anxious.

It makes me really uncomfortable; it hurts my feelings, makes me feel like there's something wrong with me.

I feel guilty for not being there like she wants me to be, angry that she won't leave my responsibilities to me or complete her own, and guilty that my depression causes her to think she has to help me out. I'm also frustrated when she lies.

Lowered self-esteem, feeling of being duped, felt really guilty a lot without knowing why.

I think this relationship turned into some sort of co-dependency. The more she affected me, the more I tried to accommodate her needs.

It causes me a lot of anxiety because we are co-workers and I can't perform at work to the fullest as she will be in the same meeting and workspace, showing the "I hate you" looks.

I'm nervous around her. She has a bad temper. We are in the same group of friends and she could "oust" me at any time.

I ended up very hurt many times. I felt used and my self-esteem dropped due to her frequent change in attitude toward me. It's hard for me to get angry, so it expresses itself as sadness. In other words, instead of getting angry with her and telling her, I became sad and took it out on myself.

I cannot be myself around her. I feel extremely self-conscious because she's always watching me ... and I know that every movement is being recorded in her pea-sized brain!

I feel like a piece of crap; I cry a lot and end up acting very needy, which I hate. I have this thing about losing her ... I guess the thought of being rejected is too painful ... yet it is a horribly painful relationship. It is not two-sided at all.

I always feel incompetent around her, like I'll never be good enough or I'm never right.

I get stressed talking to her, thinking about her, anticipating her response to me if I attempt to reach out to her. I just want her out of my life, but she keeps calling, acting like the good guy, and refusing to recognize that anything is wrong, making it look like I am the bad person because I have issues with her.

It's pissing me off, hurting me, making me angry, etc. I've put up with so much from her over the years; she has been a total bitch to all our mutual friends (introduced by me as she's such a nightmare she doesn't make many friends of her own) and now she dumps me. Hilarious!

I feel invaded, manipulated, and pressured.

I have cried more in the past year than my entire life. I feel drained, worthless, and I do not easily trust and I truly trusted her.

A bit morbid ... I kind of feel dead inside, constantly depressed.

I feel drained and confused after spending time with her. On the phone she is OK, if somewhat too much talking about herself. But when we meet in person, she puts me down, seems unhappy to see me, and brings down the situation.

It caused me a great deal of stress and frustration. I felt guilty often but also felt victimized by her which led to a downward cycle.

I felt much aggravation and disgust, I can't stand her.

I was constantly upset after talking to her, feeling like I could never please her. Whatever I did was a waste of time because she was unwilling to look at her own issues.

Terribly, I have cried so many times. The anger I have towards her has spilled out on the wrong people.

It made me feel inadequate and like I was doing something wrong.

It is completely draining, leaving me to constantly talk to others about how miserable she is making me and how I am so sick of her antics.

I would always be stressed out. I had chest pains one day and my blood pressure spiked.

It makes me question myself as a person.

I feel very depressed and trapped; it drives me to drink.

It tires me out, makes me feel drained to the point that I feel unable to think clearly enough to do school assignments. It makes me worried that things I disclosed in private will become public when she sees fit.

I lost my self-esteem for a while and stopped believing in myself.

It often made me feel sick to my stomach. I experienced a crippling devastation and was more preoccupied about that than anything else.

It's draining and I feel unsettled and "crazy" after a conversation with her.

I was extremely stressed out to the max. It seriously affected my health in a bad way. I gained weight, my hair wouldn't grow and when it did it wasn't healthy.

I was sad mainly because I was so stupid. I got taken advantage of a lot being that I am truly a nice person.

It literally made me physically ill and I became clinically depressed. I lost almost thirty pounds and had to go on antidepressants because of all the stress and strain.

I feel anxious, depressed, teary, frightened, and lonely. I know that sounds pathetic, but it really is true.

She makes me unsure of myself, my value, and my other friendships. I was happy and care-free before I met her. Now I am tense. I've had a panic attack and I feel stressed out when I'm around her.

I get pissed off and ruminate about stuff just as if she was a spouse.

My self-esteem was low. I was stressed and I gained weight from binge eating to make myself feel loved.

I allowed myself to be treated less than I would normally let people treat me. I always had an attitude towards other people because of that person.

As you can see, the negative effects of a toxic friendship can manifest themselves in many different ways. These respondents presented perfect examples of the emotional, physical, and sometimes physiological damage that can result from one's dealings with a toxic friendship. The negative feelings are real, as is the drama and trauma that these types of unhealthy relationships bring about. This should not be ignored, taken for granted, or justified by you or your toxic friend.

Grieve the Loss of the Friendship

Everyone has experienced grief during one time or another in their life. Grief is what you feel when you suffer a great loss, such as the death of a loved one or even the loss of a close friendship. The grieving process is marked by great sadness, pain, and heartache. It probably began quite some time ago when you realized your friendship was in turmoil. And now that the friendship is over, you must allow it to run its course.

Steps in the Grieving Process

Everyone grieves differently, there is no right or wrong way. However, there are some basic steps in the grieving process. Not everyone experiences the steps at the same time, and many may experience some of the steps multiple times. It's also important to understand that your grieving process may begin long before you actually end the friendship. The steps below clearly demonstrate this point. The activities that follow each step will help you determine which ones you have experienced and where you are currently in your grieving process.

Denial

At this stage, you are in awe and disbelief about what is occurring in your toxic friendship. You can't believe that your *best friend* is capable of committing such treachery against you. You are waiting to see if it could be real.

Did you experience this step?

○ Yes
○ No
○ Not Sure (but I *think* I did)

If you answered "yes" or "not sure," think about your experience and write about it in the spaces below.

_____

_____

_____

_____

_____

Heartache and Pain

The reality sets in at this point, and it feels like your heart is being shattered into a million pieces. The excruciating pain that you are experiencing is indescribable to others and it feels like you will never recover from the hurt. You may cry often and easily, and you are extremely sensitive during this time.

Did you experience this step?

- ○ Yes
- ○ No
- ○ Not Sure (but I *think* I did)

If you answered "yes" or "not sure," think about your experience and write about it in the spaces below.

_____

_____

_____

_____

_____

Anger

At this stage, you get a second reality check. Yes, she did those unfriendly things to you, and when you're finally over the initial shock and disbelief of it all, you feel really pissed off! You let her know your true feelings about her and the friendship.

Did you experience this step?

- ○ Yes
- ○ No
- ○ Not Sure (but I *think* I did)

If you answered "yes" or "not sure," think about your experience and write about it in the space below.

_____

_____

_____

_____

_____

Bargaining

You've calmed down just enough to try to figure out what went wrong and what you could do to possibly fix the problem. You may even feel guilty at some point, thinking that the negative things in the friendship are entirely your fault. You may even go to great lengths to try to save the friendship. You begin to ask yourself, *"Why me?"*

Did you experience this step?

○ Yes
○ No
○ Not Sure (but I *think* I did)

If you answered "yes" or "not sure," think about your experience and write about it in the space below.

_____

_____

_____

_____

_____

Depression

This is a time of great sadness. It occurs when you lose all hope that the friendship will ever be repaired and/or rekindled. You have gone through the denial, anger, and bargaining stages. You may express your sadness in various ways such as crying, withdrawal, or isolation.

Did you experience this step?

○ Yes
○ No
○ Not Sure (but I *think* I did)

If you answered "yes" or "not sure," think about your experience and write about it in the space below.

_____

_____

_____

_____

_____

Acceptance

Reality check! The friendship is over and now you finally accept it. It's time to move on with your life. The sadness may still be there on some level but it no longer dictates how you live your life. And as times passes, the intensity of the sadness decreases. However, for some, it may never _completely_ go away.
Did you experience this step?

- ○ Yes
- ○ No
- ○ Not Sure (but I _think_ I did)

If you answered "yes" or "not sure," think about your experience and write about it in the space below.

_____

_____

_____

_____

_____

Facts about Grieving

- Crying is a normal part of grieving; it's not a sign of personal weakness.
- You'll have good days and bad days while grieving. It's an emotional roller-coaster ride.
- Talking about your loss is a necessary and good thing.
- Moving on with your life means you have accepted the loss but not forgotten about it.

Myths about Grieving

- The pain will go away if you ignore it.
- Everyone grieves the loss of the same thing.

- Everyone grieves in the same way.
- Everyone experiences the stages of grief in the same sequence as others.
- Grief is a sign of weakness.
- It has a specified time frame.

What Others Don't Understand

It may be difficult for some people to understand why you would grieve the loss of a toxic friendship that once caused you so much pain. But grieving does happen, and when it does, victims must allow the process to take place. Grief is very personal, so the way you grieve is going to be different than how someone else might grieve the same type of loss. Your period of grief may be longer or shorter than someone else's. It may be more or less intense than others' grief, due to the same causes. Nevertheless, it's *your* grief and you must not allow others to dictate how you should experience it or prevent it from running its course in your life. Remember, if emotional freedom is your goal, remain vigilant and you will recover from this.

Toxic Friendship Survivors

Toxic friendship survivors have been burned once and perhaps even twice, so they have the wherewithal to recognize a toxic friendship and deal with it accordingly. There are two types of toxic friendship survivors:

- True
- Simulated

True Survivors

True Survivors are those who walked away and stayed away from their toxic friendships. They didn't look back or second-guess their motives for recognizing and ending it even if it took numerous attempts to do so. They have learned to live their life without their FTF. All potential friends are carefully evaluated. And the cultivation of any new friendship comes to a screeching halt if the potential friend exhibits any signs of toxicity. *True Survivors* have been there and done that and are well aware of the ill effects and consequences of *waiting to see* if the toxic behaviors of a potential friend will either cease to exist or improve.

The Ones Who Walk Away

- End their toxic friendship.
- Go through the healing process.
- Grieve the loss of the friendship.
- Forgive the perpetrator.
- Regain their peace of mine.
- Have no feelings of guilt or regret.
- Never look back.
- Move on with their life.
- Are toxic friendship free.

Facts about True Survivors

They ...

- Know the ill effects and consequences of ignoring the red flags of a toxic friendship.
- Know how to recognize a toxic friendship and thus avoid them.
- Know how to ignore the seemingly rational thoughts that may pop into their heads such as "*She is a really nice person, but ...*" or "*We have a lot in common, but ...*"
- Have been burned once by a toxic friend, so they have learned from their experience.
- Don't wait around to see if a new friend is going to stop or change her questionable behaviors.
- Immediately take action at any signs of toxicity in their friendships, even if it means ending it.

- Don't waste valuable time and energy trying to figure out ways to change their own behavior to accommodate the wants/needs of the perpetrator.
- Pay close attention to the red flags and warning signs of a potentially toxic friendship.
- Don't let their feelings about a new friendship impede their efforts to think rationally about the situation.
- Realize that if there's a "*but*" added to every nice thing they have to say or think about a person, they had better think twice about cultivating a friendship with her.
- Know that the "*buts*" will come back to haunt them once they realize how toxic their friend is.
- Are unmoved by the wooing and pleading of their toxic friend, and her declarations of "*I really didn't mean any harm,*" "*It won't happen again,*" or "*You're my best friend,*" etc.

Simulated Survivors

Simulated Survivors remain in their toxic friendships for various reasons, but also gain the knowledge and survival skills (see Appendix 1) needed to cope with the perpetrator. They develop effective ways of maintaining their relationships, which takes a lot of effort. This only occurs when the victims feel their toxic friendships are *really* worth saving. And they believe that every effort they make towards succeeding at an overwhelming task will make their life much more pleasant and the perpetrator more tolerable. Although they don't end their toxic friendship completely, they still have to cope.

Simulated Survivors have to deal with the reality that their friendship will never be the same again.

The Ones Who Stay

- Remain in their toxic friendships but do so with caution.
- Develop effective ways of dealing with the perpetrator.
- Work very hard at maintaining their unhealthy friendship.
- Know when to temporarily back away from the perpetrator.

- Have knowledge which helps them deal/cope with their toxic friend.
- Have built an outside support system.

Facts about Simulated Survivors

They ...
- Have difficulty regaining trust in the perpetrator.
- Know they cannot force the perpetrator to change her negative behaviors.
- Know the type of toxic friend they have and thus deal with her accordingly.
- Are always on edge about the friendship.
- Decrease their dependency on the friendship.
- Handle the perpetrator with a long handle spoon.

Whether you choose to end a toxic friendship or remain in it, dealing with the perpetrator is truly a feat of survival. And only when you are armed with the knowledge of the *What? When? Why? or How?*, of toxic people; will you begin to understand their behavior. Knowledge is power, and it is the ultimate weapon to use when you find yourself doing battle with a toxic friend.

Self-Evaluation

Think about the goals for your toxic friendship. What do you want to be? A ...

- ○ True Survivor
- ○ Simulated Survivor
- ○ I don't know yet

If you decide to remain in your toxic friendship, be vigilant in your efforts to not let it control your life.

AVOIDING TOXIC FRIENDSHIPS

Reality *Check*

Choosing the right adulthood friends is just as important; if not more, than when we chose our childhood friends. Heed the warnings given to us by the wise adults in our childhood lives and proceed with great caution and care when cultivating adulthood friendships.

Knowledge is Power

*K*nowledge is no doubt one of the best weapons to use when dealing with toxic friends, as well as when you're trying to avoid them. Educating yourself about the various types of toxic friends is important, but there are also some other things that you must do to avoid falling prey to a toxic friendship.

Here are a few of them ...

- Recognize the early red flags and don't ignore them, especially the subtle ones.
- Ask a potential friend some of the same types of questions you would ask a potential boyfriend or mate.
- Nip the negativity and the nonsense in the bud before you develop a close intimate bond with your friend.
- Know who you are, respect yourself, and keep your self-esteem in check.
- Set clear, concise, and easily identifiable personal boundaries. Maintain them no matter what.

In addition to all of these things, we must also remember the lessons taught by our parents, guardians, and other knowledgeable adults who tried their best to steer us away from unhealthy youthful friendships.

Choosing Adulthood Friends

Do you remember growing up and your parents and/or other adults telling you to be careful who you choose to be your friends? They warned us about the trouble-makers and the ones who made bad or inappropriate choices. Although we didn't want to hear the warnings from our parents (after all, what did they know?), we somehow had brief moments of reason and realized that our parents' advice during that time was not only reasonable, but necessary for us to evolve into sane adults.

But with all that wonderful advice given to us by our parents, did they ever warn us to be careful about how we choose our adulthood friends? Probably not, so here we are living our adult lives and wondering how we ended up with a toxic friendship.

As an addendum to the advice given to us by our parents when we were children:

We must all be careful about who we choose to be our adulthood friends as well!!!

Yes, even as adults, we must really be cautious. Why? In most instances, we do not have a clue about the background of the adults we allow into our hearts, our lives, our families, our homes, etc. Adults who have unresolved problems and issues from their childhood, teenage years, or early and even later adulthood will no doubt bring those issues into the friendship on some level. And those things will certainly have a negative impact on the relationship that you develop with them.

What to Consider When Choosing Adulthood Friends

- Intellectual capacity and/or ability
- Financial stability and/or lack of

- Employment status
- Housing/living arrangements
- Level of education
- Status of parenthood
- Interests and/or lack of
- Religious and/or spiritual beliefs
- Other beliefs as well as personal values
- Level of independence and/or lack of
- Quality of health
- Marital or relationship status
- Social status
- Criminal history and/or background if any
- Mental health and/or psychological state of mind

Although this is not an inclusive list of things you should consider when choosing adulthood friends, it is a good start. If any one or more of these entities are imbalanced in a friendship, a toxic situation could occur as you may find yourself compensating for what your friend is lacking or being caught in the middle of her drama and issues.

Tips for Making New Friends

Despite the negativity of a current or former toxic friendship, most people want to have at least one or more close healthy friendships. However, after ending a toxic friendship, one might be reluctant to add new people to their friendship list. Even though we don't want to enter any new friendship thinking it may be another toxic one, victims can't help but think about the possibility of a repeat negative experience.

There are no guarantees that a friendship will be healthy or even toxic, but past negative experiences *should* warn us to be cautious of anyone who wants to enter into our friendship circle after an experience with a FTF. It is better to be safe than sorry; therefore, one should be very careful about selecting their new friends. The following are a few suggestions to help guide you in your selection of new friends subsequent to experiencing a toxic friendship.

Evaluating Potential Friends

Familiarize yourself with the various types of toxic friends. There are many different types and your potential friend can exhibit the characteristics of several of them. And be on the lookout for the warning signs of a toxic friendship. In many cases, the warning signs are there but they are so subtle that we often don't recognize them or simply choose to ignore them. Sometimes you won't detect the toxicity at the onset of the friendship because the toxic friend will make a great effort to convince you that she is a loyal and trustworthy friend.

When your intuition tells you that something is not right at the onset of a new friendship, pay attention and check it out. Realize that something has been revealed to you and indicates that you may not want to proceed with cultivating that particular relationship.

When in Doubt, Check Her Out

When you rid yourself of a toxic friendship and began your search for a healthy one, the first thing you'll want to know is whether or not the new friend will be toxic. Unfortunately, there is no crystal ball that will reveal such information to you. But now that you have learned what toxic friendships are and how to recognize them, you can use that knowledge in conjunction with your common sense to help lessen the changes of falling prey once again.

Ways to Check Her Out

- Observation
- Indirect Questioning
- Direct Questioning

Observation

Carefully observe the behaviors, actions, and reactions of your potential friend. If you pay close attention, you may be able to identify potentially toxic behaviors. If your instinct tells you that something isn't right, don't ignore it!

Tips for Observing Your Potential Friend

- Be discrete and don't tell her that she is being observed.
- If possible, try to set up scenarios that might elicit certain behaviors, actions, or reactions.
- Look for consistency or inconsistencies in her behavior, actions, or reactions.
- If you continue to have any doubts or concerns after observing your potential friend, start asking her some questions.

Indirect Questioning

In some cases, you may not be able to find out what you need to know just by observing your potential friend. If that's the case, you may have to resort to questioning her to find out what you need to know. Indirect questioning is a good way to start because this type of questioning is meant to be more polite while appearing to be less intrusive. Although the goal is to find out what you need to know, your potential friend will be less likely to take offense to this type of questioning.

Tips for Using Indirect Questioning

- Always start with a polite comment.
- Make your questions long and drawn out.
- Add a little humor, if possible.
- Integrate your questions into your general conversations with your potential friend.

Sample Questions

- I recently ended a toxic friendship. Have you ever been involved with one?

- I once had a friend who was really depressed. Are you familiar with the signs of depression?
- People with low self-esteem often have a difficult time in relationships. Do you know how to recognize a person who has low self-esteem?
- Mary has been my friend for many years. Do you have any long-term friendships?
- I really like my career as a lawyer. How do you feel about your career?
- I only like driving SUVs. What type of cars do you like to drive?
- TV police stories can be really intense. Have you ever had any direct experience with the police?

Direct Questioning

Direct questioning is more intrusive than indirect questioning. Your potential friend may very well take offense to this type of questioning and possibly be reluctant to pursue a friendship with you. But you must do what is necessary to protect yourself from a potentially toxic friendship. The damage that a toxic friendship can do to you is far worse than a potential friend getting offended by your questions. You need to know whether or not this new person in your life is going to be a good fit or wreak havoc. It's best to be cautious, rather than being too quick to befriend.

Tips for Using Direct Questioning

- Use this type of questioning only if you can't find out what you need to know from observation or indirect questioning.
- Understand the risks; your potential friend may be turned off by such questioning.
- Don't be afraid to ask what you need or want to know, and don't beat around the bush.
- Ask questions based on your past experience with a toxic friendship.

- Consider your personal beliefs and expectations of what a healthy friendship should be.
- If your potential friend refuses to answer any of your questions or becomes offended by them, that could signal a red flag – but not necessarily.
- If she truly wants to be your friend, then understanding your need to ask certain questions is a must. If she doesn't understand, then you might want to reconsider developing a friendship with her.

Sample Questions

- How often do you change friends?
- Are you depressed or have you ever suffered from clinical depression?
- How is your self-esteem?
- Do you currently have a job?
- Do you own a car?
- Do you have a criminal record?

Why Such Questioning?

These questions may seem a little intrusive to some but again it is better to be cautious than quick to befriend. If you encounter a potentially toxic friend, keep in mind that you can't change her behavior. And more than likely, she has no intentions of changing it herself, even if this means not beginning a new friendship with you – let alone maintaining it. If you feel you really want to develop a close friendship with a potentially toxic friend, be willing to change *your* behavior in order to deal or cope with her. But before you can do that, you must first find out whom and what you're dealing with. One way to do so is to ask questions in order to gain information about what you *don't* know or what you *need* to know.

If your potential friend is unwilling to answer any of your questions (and that may certainly be the case), see if you can find out what you need to know from other sources such as mutual friends, co-workers, neighbors, classmates, etc.; however, do so with caution. Some people may be willing to share information with you while others may not. Either way, it's certainly worth trying if you have suspicions, concerns, or doubts about your potential friend. But keep this in mind, if your potential friend learns that you are trying to gather information about her from other sources; she may take offense and halt the cultivation of the friendship with you. That's the chance you will take if you decide to go this route.

Things You Should *Not* Do When You Meet a New Friend

Just like an apple tree, it takes time to grow a friendship. The seed must be planted and given the right care so that it will sprout, grow into a fruitful tree, and not wither away and die from neglect. And just like an apple tree, a new relationship must be given the proper care as it progresses from being an acquaintanceship to a healthy and happy friendship.

Keeping those thoughts in mind, here are just few things you might want to avoid doing when you meet a potential friend:

Don't be fooled by a friendly smile or too many acts of kindness, as those could be indicators of what's yet to come.

Don't allow her to cross your personal boundary lines. If she does it once and you don't bring it to her attention, she'll assume it's OK and continue to do so until you nip it in the bud.

Don't pretend to be something you're not. If you start off being a fake, you'll have to work hard at trying to maintain the façade. If you have a certain personality, don't change it just because it doesn't fit the manifesto of your new friend.

Don't change who you are just to please her.

Don't sacrifice your individuality.

Don't lose your independence or become dependent on a new friendship.

Don't *humble yourself to the point where you begin to lose sight of who you are and she begins to take advantage of you. It's OK to be nice to your new friend, but … just be careful.*

Don't *act desperate or lonely for her friendship. Such behavior makes you an easy target for the user, charmer, swindler, etc. If she thinks you are in desperate need for a friend, she will detect it and take advantage of it if she has a toxic mentality.*

Don't *agree with everything she says, does, or wants. If you cater to her too often, she'll consider you easy prey and will expect you to maintain your agreeable disposition at all times.*

Don't *loan her money. If you do so often and freely, she will expect you to do it each and every time she asks. You will become her personal cash machine, and the more you loan her, the less you'll get back.*

Don't *be her taxi service or let her borrow your car. Don't be so willing to chauffer her around or let her have your car keys. Don't be too generous, just because you enjoy her companionship or don't mind letting her use your car because she doesn't have one. She will expect you to continue the deed throughout the friendship and will avoid seeking other means of transportation because she has deemed you her personal limo service and you have graciously played the part.*

Don't *help her find a job at your place of employment. We all want to help our friends; however, you could be setting yourself up for a lot of drama or hurt and pain. What if your friend turns out to be a toxic one, then what? What if she steals the spotlight from you, or better yet, your promotion? What if there's conflict in the friendship and you decide to end it, then what? It's not easy to go to work and sit right next to the person who was once your best friend but is now your worst enemy.*

Don't *get in the habit of buying things for her that she can buy for herself but is too cheap to do so. She will always have an excuse as to why she can't do for herself.*

Don't *let her know how much the friendship means to you; she could misinterpret it to mean that you will do just about anything to maintain the friendship with her – again, making you an easy target.*

Don't tell her all of your secrets (keep some to yourself). This could backfire on you. She could later use them as a way of controlling you and the friendship.

Don't tell her too much of your personal business; keep some things private.

Don't give her keys to your home. If the friendship ends, you may have to change all of your locks because she won't give back the keys or you simply don't trust her anymore.

Don't give her keys to your heart; she may cause irreparable damage.

Don't be her problem-solver. If you solve one, she's going to expect you to solve them all.

Don't be available at her beck and call and allow her to monopolize your time and energy. Don't answer all of her phone calls, texts, and emails right away, even if she gets upset.

Don't discuss important personal information, such as your income, financial situation, your marriage, or your relationship with a significant other, etc.

Don't introduce her to your immediate family. You may speak about her to them but don't be so quick to invite her into your family life.

Don't allow yourself to become her free babysitter, run errands for her, or become her personal flunky.

Don't be her personal chef and cook meals for her and her family.

Don't be her therapist, doctor, or lawyer by offering too much friendly advice or helping her solve too many of her own problems; she will become dependent on that.

Don't allow her to try and change who you are; try to maintain your sense of self and independence.

Don't be a people pleaser and try to cater to her every want, need, and/or desire.

Don't always go where she wants to go or do what she wants to do.

Don't answer all of the personal questions that she may ask you (some stuff is none of her business).

Don't start a business with her, especially if you really don't know her and what her true motives are.

Don't try to be her parent, surrogate, or act as a significant other.

Don't help her do things that she should be doing for herself, but won't; because she knows you will do them for her.

Don't use her for your own personal gain.

Don't feel obligated to do anything for her.

Things You *Should* Do When You Meet a New Friend

Doing a few bold things prior to developing a close bond or connection with a potential friend can save you from getting trapped within the confines of a toxic friendship. It isn't always easy to free yourself once you are emotionally trapped. So it's better to be cautious in the beginning, rather than trapped in the middle – at which point you are contemplating whether you will ever see the end because sometimes it's simply too hard to let go. Taking a few bold steps could prevent you from becoming the victim of a toxic friendship in the first place.

Here are just a few things you should do when you met a potential friend:

Do be cautious rather than careless; most new friends are strangers.

Do be yourself, not who your friend wants you to be or thinks you already are.

Do be honest and communicate your feelings and any concerns you may have.

Do state your expectations of the friendship and discuss the criterion for a healthy and satisfying friendship with you.

Do ask important and sometimes intrusive questions.

Do set clear and concise boundaries right away.

Do say "No"; say it early on and make it stick.

Do check your level of self-esteem.

Do *ask yourself whether or not this person is a right fit for your life.*

Do *learn all that you can about unhealthy friendships.*

Do *follow your gut instincts and intuition.*

Do *judge a book by its cover, sometimes that's all you have to go by.*

Do *a Self-Evaluation and inventory. Ask yourself why you are looking to create a new friendship. What personal need are you trying to fill – loneliness, companionship, someone to use or take advantage of?*

Do *befriend someone only for the right reasons.*

Do *maintain your own personality and individuality.*

Do *a "needs assessment". Find out what your potential friend is looking for in a friendship. What are her expectations? Is she looking for a casual relationship, close friendship, rebound/replacement friend, etc.?*

In addition, view your relationship with your toxic friend as a learning experience not just a toxic connection. The lessons learned will help you make better friendship choices in the future and/or make necessary changes in your current friendships. You can also use your knowledge and experience to help others who may be oblivious to what they're dealing with in their own friendships...remember knowledge is power!

Below are a few of the lessons victims learned from their toxic friendships:

> *Get out as soon as you realize something is wrong because the longer you stay in the friendship the harder it will be to end it.*

> *Think less of what other people are trying to do, be less emotional about it, and walk away and do my own thing – it's their loss. I was a good friend who would've walked many miles to help them - but not anymore.*

> *Sometimes we are better off without having a best friend at all rather than being involved in a toxic relationship.*

Pay attention to your instincts. I had a feeling early on that she was toxic but I ignored my own intuition and remained friends with her for four years. It would have been easier to end it if I would have paid attention to my instincts and ended things earlier.

I learned that you can never meet the perfect friend, not even in church. And to never disclose a certain part of myself to certain people because they may use it against me.

The way you start a friendship has a lot to do with what you deal with later on. Don't make behavior that is unacceptable, acceptable because you feel sorry for someone or you think you can save or change them.

You can't fix people. They can only fix themselves. In the end, you do have to look out for number one. Don't hang around hoping things will change. It's not worth it.

Do not give your heart to a person; always leave a room for disappointment.

Friendship must be a two-way thing. It should never make you unhappy and eat away at your self-esteem.

Stand your ground – you can't be walked on if you don't volunteer yourself to be a personal doormat!

You don't have to take on their crap; a real friend doesn't make you squirm and delight in it.

Be leery of people who appear in your life, suddenly call themselves your BFF, and then turn everyday life into a TV drama.

Not everyone will add value to my life and it made me a stronger person and more self-confident because I knew I deserved better.

Wise up, move on, and don't put up with shit – value yourself more than that!

If I have doubts about a friend from the start, I need to listen to my gut and not start a friendship. That way, I will be saving myself from a lot of anxiety and sadness in the future.

Life is too short to have nasty, negative people in your life. Friendship should be about fun, understanding, and have mutual respect. It should be consistent when you're feeling great and also when you are down.

Trust my instincts and never let a person treat me like that again. Realize that I am worthy and don't deserve to be treated poorly.

Confront the issue sooner rather than later because if left unresolved it can have far reaching negative impacts on your life.

I have learned how important it is to stick up for yourself and let people know when their behavior is affecting you negatively, especially when it comes to your mental health. If I had done that from the beginning, I may have been able to keep my friendship from becoming toxic.

Set boundaries early on in the friendship and don't let their 'flattery' get the better of you. Toxic friends play on your 'soft side' and use it to take advantage of your good nature. They choose their victims and are natural 'players' in intimidation and exploitation of them. They 'mess' with your mind and make you feel like you're the guilty party and that you're the crazy one.

Self-Evaluation

What steps have you taken to evaluate any new friendships beyond your toxic one?

List them in the space below.

_____

_____

_____

_____

_____

Conclusion

*O*ftentimes, the victim of a toxic friendship finds herself playing a very dangerous and emotional game called *"Wait and See."* The object of the game is to wait for the perpetrator to change her negative or inappropriate behavior(s). The pawns of the game are the broken pieces of the victim's heart, which she strategically tries to piece together after each upset and then claim victory at winning the game over and over again.

The most challenging obstacle of the *"Wait and See"* game is that no matter how skilled the victim is at displaying *patience, tolerance,* and *understanding,* she can never truly win unless she walks away. That's because it's a game that requires the victim and the perpetrator to agree upon a mutually accepted behavior within the friendship. Unfortunately, the perpetrator usually doesn't have the skills, knowledge, or willingness to play the game fairly.

Sometimes it's difficult to know whether or not a seemingly healthy friendship will turn toxic if you are not familiar with the red flags. Sometimes your friend's behavior might be mistaken for something else. However, if you are forewarned and educated about toxic friendships, you can train your brain to be on the lookout for any signs of toxicity in your current or future friendships. And then deal with them accordingly, no matter how much hurt and pain it causes.

Sometimes you have to walk away and stay away from the people and things you love …

Then love them at a distance …

It's a hard thing to do, but with time and patience … it can be done.

And always remember this…

Friendship is a relationship of *choice*, so choose wisely and don't let your emotions guide your friendship choices.

FRIENDSHIP RULES
IMPORTANT COMMUNICATION NOTES
TOXIC FRIENDSHIP DETOXIFICATION
SURVIVAL SKILLS FOR SIMULATORS

Friendships Rules

Ten Rules of Friendship That Protect Your Friend

1. Don't reveal your friend's secrets or confidences to others, and don't say bad or negative things about your friend behind her back.
2. Always be there for her, through the good times as well as the bad.
3. Respect your friend as a person, not her title, status, assets, or what she can do for you.
4. Don't make promises you can't keep or have no intentions of keeping.
5. Don't be a Naysayer; instead, be hopeful and optimistic about your friend's goals and aspirations.
6. Always be truthful and honest to your friend.
7. Never take your friend for granted or take advantage of her kindness. Be grateful and always show appreciation.
8. Accept your friend for who she is and don't try to change her. If you can't deal with who she is as a person, then move on.
9. Don't fool around with your friend's significant other.
10. Respect all boundaries set by your friend, even if you don't agree with them and respect her right to privacy.

Ten Rules of Friendship That Protect You

1. Don't allow your friend to control you or the friendship; take a stand on things that make you feel uncomfortable.
2. Don't allow your friend to persuade you to do things that are not in your best physical, emotional, financial, or spiritual interest.
3. Stick to your morals and principles, and don't allow your friend to persuade you to change or violate them.
4. Maintain a sense of self and individuality no matter how close the bond of friendship is.

5. Don't become overly dependent on your friend for companionship or anything else.
6. Expect reciprocity. If it is not present then demand it. And if it is not given, consider ending the friendship.
7. Don't allow your friend to silence you; speak your mind.
8. Learn to say "No" and not feel guilty about doing so.
9. Set personal boundaries, and don't allow your friend to cross them.
10. Don't tell your friend everything; keep some things to yourself.

Important Communication Notes

Choose a method for communicating your intentions of ending a toxic friendship (see Chapter 7).

After you have let your toxic friend know your intentions, need you say more? No, move forward but proceed with caution. It may be difficult but *try* not to look back.

- Avoid overreacting to your friend's response(s). She may become angry or upset but don't let her behavior dictate or manipulate yours.
- Avoid any type of violence when communicating with her.
- Avoid the use of profanity and obscenities.
- Avoid blaming or accusing your friend. This is not the time to do so. Instead, use lots of "I" statements. This is about *you* and how *you* feel – not your friend.
- Avoid using ambiguous language. Get to the point, and make it clear and concise.

Toxic Friendship Detoxification

The process of emotionally removing a toxic friend from your life is what I like to call "Toxic Friendship Detoxification." It is defined as the process in which one focuses on their own emotional healing and self-rediscovery either alone or with the help of others (friends, relatives, mental health care professionals, etc.) to overcome the emotional and psychological dependence on their toxic friend's companionship.

It's not an easy transformation from being best friends today to strangers tomorrow. You may have some doubts and second thoughts about it sometimes. This can be a very painful and tough decision. You may be able to physically remove your friend from your presence but that is only the beginning. Making the decision to walk away leads you down a sometimes very dark and lonely road in life and emotional recovery without your toxic friend. However, the following detoxification process can make the journey a little shorter and the road a lot smoother.

How to Detox

Use a JOT

If you haven't done so already, start a Journal of Toxicity (JOT). It will serve as a constant reminder and confirmation of why it was necessary to end your toxic friendship. Use it to write down your feelings each day or the encounters you may have with your friend, if any. You can also use it as a way to keep track of your progress or lack of. At some point, you will be able to look back at your JOT with awe and disbelief at how you allowed yourself to put up with the nonsense for so long. And that's a really good feeling!

Forgive Your Friend

When you are READY, forgive your friend for all that you feel she has done to you (see Chapter 9). And don't do it because it's the right thing to do. You must do it when you can sincerely mean it and not just as a formality. However, keep in mind that you won't be able to truly begin your healing process until you've forgiven her but that this should not have any impact on your decision to end the friendship and detoxify her from your life. And when you do forgive her, also keep in mind that forgiving doesn't mean forgetting.

Identify Your Role

Take a good look at the role you played in your toxic friendship. Acknowledge any negative behaviors and/or mistakes you may have made. Then learn from them. Avoid duplicating them in your current healthy friendships or any future ones.

Fight the Urges

Avoid urges to make contact with the perpetrator, if you have eliminated the toxic friendship from your life – this will only set you back. When you feel the urge to call or visit her, make contact with someone else instead. Keep a list of numbers and addresses handy and use them. It may help to elicit a couple of supporters who will be there when you need them at a moment's notice.

Seek Support

Create a support system of other friends, relatives, co-workers, significant other, etc. Let them know that you are detoxifying from the perpetrator, and you need the support of individuals who will allow you to express your feelings and concerns without judgment or criticism. Your support system should consist of people who are genuinely concerned about your emotional well-being.

Engage in Mind Sweeping

This is when you remove all tangible reminders of your friend, such as pictures, gifts, clothing, mementos, etc. You can return them all, donate them to charity, burn them, throw them in the trash, or just remove them from your sight until you decide what to do with them at a later date. You can remove all the items at one time or you can do one or more at a time, depending on your comfort level. However, the sooner you do this the better.

Grieve the Loss

Allow yourself to grieve the loss of the friendship by familiarizing yourself with the grieving process. (see Chapter 9)

Get Help

Seek professional help if needed; don't be ashamed or embarrassed. If talking to a therapist or clergy person is the only way you feel you can weather this emotional storm, then do it. Don't beat yourself down to the point where you cannot pick yourself up *alone*. If the friendship has caused you to fall into a deep state of the depression, you may very well need the help of a professional to dig you out.

Restructure Your Time

Get involved in an activity or volunteer your free time, the time you would have normally spent with your friend. Try something new rather than something you once did with your friend, the old things would only bring back memories which you may not be ready for at this time.

Be Cautious and Patient

Avoid searching for a rebound or replacement friend. Give yourself time to heal and rediscover who you are as an individual before trying to cultivate a new friendship. You will have plenty of time for that. In many instances, one may search but never find a friend to take the place of their old toxic one. But you will eventually develop new friendships if that's what you seek.

Rediscover Yourself

Who are you as an individual? What is the purpose for your life, and how can you fulfill that purpose? What can you do to become a better person? There are many questions you can ask yourself. What are you waiting for?

Survival Skills for Simulators

- Learn to say "**No**" and make it stick.
- Don't take ownership of your toxic friend's issues and problems.
- Maintain a high level of self-esteem.
- Pick and choose your battles, but nip the nonsense in the bud.
- Maintain your individuality and don't lose sight of yourself.
- Keep your gullibility level in check.
- Lower your friendship expectations.
- Set and maintain boundaries.
- Don't suppress your discontent with your friend's negative behaviors; talk about it.
- Don't ignore your instincts.
- Give yourself permission to end the friendship, if you no longer feel like you want to maintain it.

RESOURCES FOR VICTIMS, SURVIVORS, AND PERPETRATORS

Other Writings by Loraine Smith-Hines

If you would like to read more of the author's writings, please visit *www.toxicfriendships.org*

Recommended Reading/Bibliography

Books

Baker, Elizabeth. *Living With Eeyore: How To Positively Love The Negative People In Your Life.* Cincinnati, Ohio: Standard Publishing Company, 2007.

Bernstein, Albert. *Emotional Vampires: Dealing With People Who Drain You Dry.* New York: McGraw Hill, 2001.

Bucklin, Linda & Keil, Mary. *Come Rain Or Come Shine: Friendships Between Women.* Holbrook, Mass: Adams Media Corporation, 1999.

Eng, Karen. *Secrets & Confidences: The Complicated Truth About Women's Friendship.* Emeryville, CA: Seal Press, 2004.

Glass, Lillian PhD. *Toxic People: 10 Ways Of Dealing With People Who Make Your Life Miserable. New York:* St. Martin's Press, 1997.

Grant, Ruthie O. PhD. *I Thought I Was The Crazy One: 201 Ways To Identify And Deal With Toxic People.* Fawnskin, CA: Personhood Press, 2003.

Green, Jane Dr & Rosen, Margaret D. *How Could You Do This to Me? Learning To Trust After Betrayal.* New York: Broadway Books, 1997.

Isaacs, Florence. *Toxic Friends True Friends: How Your Friendships Can Make Or Break Your Health, Happiness, Family, And Career.* Citadel: 2003.

McLemore, Clinton W. Dr. *Toxic Relationships and How To Change Them: Health And Holiness In Everyday Life.* San Francisco: Jossey-Bass, 2003.

Pryor, Liz. *What Did I Do Wrong? When Women Don't Tell Each Other The Friendship Is Over.* New York: Free Press, 2006.

Wickwire, Jeff. *Friendships: Avoiding The Ones That Hurt, Finding The Ones That Heal.* Grand Rapids, Michigan: Chosen Books, 2007.

Yager, Jan. *Friendshifts: The Power Of Friendship And How It Shapes Our Lives.* Stamford, Connecticut: Hannacroix Books, Inc., 1999.

Yager, Jan. *When Friendship Hurts: How To Deal With Friends Who Betray, Abandon, Or Wound You.* New York: Fireside, 2002.

Web Articles

Borden, Debra. "Toxic Friends." http://www.debraborden.com/blog/2006/09/toxicfriends.html

Breyer, Amelia. "Do You Have A Toxic Friend? 8 Toxic Friends To Identify." http://www.associatedcontent.com

Bromstein, Elizabeth. "How To Kiss Off A Friendship: Breaking A Bad Bond With A Bud Is Harder Than Ending A Love Tie." http://www.nowtoronto.com/issues/2007-09-27/goodshealth.php

Dunn, Darlene. "Take Inventory Of Friends; Is One Toxic?" http://www.newsnet5.com/News/1403356/detail.html

Ehmann, Lain. "Now It's Time To Say Goodbye: Ending Friendships."
http://www.swedish.org/17425.cfm

Hatfield, Heather. "Toxic Friends: Less Friend, More Foe."
http://www.webmd.com/features/toxic-friends-less-friend-more-foe?print=true

Kane, Esther. "Saying No To Toxic Relationships."
www.articlesfactory.com/articles/womens-issues/saying-no-to-toxic-relationships.html

Mandel, Debbie. "How To Recognize And Shed Toxic Friends."
http://www.chetday.com/badfriends.htm

McHugh, Beth. "Do You Have A Toxic Friend?"
http://www.mental-health.families.com/blog/do-you-have-toxic-friend

McLendon, Sibyl. "Toxic Friendships.".
http://www.articlesfactory.com/articles/motivational/toxic-friendships.html

Nelson, DJ. "5 Signs Of A Toxic Friend."
http://www.ezinearticles.com/?5-signs-of-a-Toxic Friend&id=689756

Paries, Rinatta. "Setting Boundaries In Relationships." Sept. 2001. http://www.onlineorganizing.com

Piderman, Katherine M. PhD. "Forgiveness: How To Let Go Of Grudges And Bitterness." 4 Nov. 2008.
http://www.mayoclinic.com/health/forgiveness/MH00131

Pratt, Catherine. "How To Deal With Negative People."
http://www.life-with-confidence.com/how-to-deal-with-negative-people.html

Pratt, Catherine. "Unhealthy Friendships: Why Do We Keep Them?"
http://www.life-with-confidence.com/unhealthy-friendships.html

Saltz, Gail Dr. "Is Your Friendship Not Working? Here's Help." http://www.msnbc.msn.com/id/21411233/

Wald, Deborah. "Don't Keep It All Bottled Up." http://www. healthyplace.com/Communities/Relationships/Site/toxic_rela- tionships.htm

Websites

"Common Negative Feelings." http://www.eqi.org/cnfs.htm

"Dealing With Manipulative People." 27 Apr. 2006. http://www.lifehack.org/articles/lifehack/dealing-with-manipu- lative-people.html

"Friendships." http://www.ag.org/top/Beliefs/relations_14_friendships.cfm

"How Can I Tell If A Friendship Is Unhealthy?" www.christianitytoday.com/biblestudies/questions/friendsun- healthy2.html

"How To Handle Difficult People." www.essortment.com/all/howtohandleedi_riuu.htm

"How To Handle Toxic Friends." http://www.cbsnews.com/stories/2006/01/26/health/webmd/ printable1242335.shtml/

"Toxic Friends–Toxic Friendships: When Friends Hurt And Friendships Harm." http://www.cyberparent.com/friendship/toxic-friends- friendship.htm

Glossary

Abuser – Toxic friend who is verbally, physically, emotionally, or sexually abusive.

Accuser – Toxic friend who blames you for all the problems, issues, and drama in her life.

Acquaintance – Someone you know slightly rather than intimately.

Addict – Toxic friend who is physically and/or psychologically dependent on a substance, behavior, or activity which causes her to behave compulsively or obsessively.

Advisor – Toxic friend who analyzes everything you do and constantly gives unwanted advice.

Arrogant – Very conceited and stuck up toxic friend who has an extremely high level of pride and thinks she is better than everyone else.

Attention Seekers – Category of toxic friends who thrive off the attention of others and don't care whether the attention is positive or negative.

Avoiders – Category of toxic friends who always wheedle their way out responsibility, accountability, or sticky and uncomfortable situations.

Best Friend Forever – The friend you hope will be your best friend now and forever.

Betrayer – Toxic friend who double-crosses you and betrays your trust in one way or another. What you consider betrayal is up to you.

BFF – Acronym for *best friend forever*.

Blame Game – Psychological trick used when your friend doesn't want to take responsibility or be held accountable for her behaviors and actions.

Busy Body Big Mouths – Category of toxic friends who constantly run their mouths.

Caretaker – Excessively nurturing toxic friend who acts like your parent and has a strong desire to care for your wants and needs while neglecting her own.

Charlatans – Category of toxic friends who like to play games of deception and are masters at the craft of making you believe they are truly something they're not.

Charmer – Very charismatic and charming toxic friend who starts off a friendship by presenting herself as one of the nicest people you've ever met (but later her true colors come to light).

Cheater – Rule breaking toxic friend who flirts, messes around with, or steals your romantic partner.

Clueless – Toxic friend who lacks common sense and the ability to learn or even understand the simplest things.

Competitor – Toxic friend who finds joy in constantly competing against you because she wants everything you have and tries to take it all away from you.

Complainer – Toxic friend who gripes and complains excessively about almost anything and everything.

Control Freaks – Category of toxic friends who like to boss you around, tell you what to do, how to do it, when to do it, and who to do it with.

Copycat – Toxic friend who imitates and copies everything you do; she wants to be like you.

Covert – Something that is done secretly or undercover.

Criticizer – Extremely critical toxic friend who finds fault in everything you do.

Daredevil – Risk-taking toxic friend who does things that puts herself or others in danger or harm's way.

Defender – Toxic friend who won't let you fight your own battles because she doesn't feel you're capable of doing so yourself.

Direct Questioning – These types of questions are direct and to the point and can be answered with a simple "yes" or "no".

Doctor – Toxic friend who likes to use her lay medical knowledge to diagnosis and treat every ailment you may have.

Double Talker – Toxic friend who likes to use ambiguous language and confusing talk, in an effort to leave you confused, baffled, and in the dark.

Drama Queen – Melodramatic toxic friend who is highly emotional and makes a drama out of every situation in her life.

Ego Trippers – Category of toxic friends who are only concerned about their own well-being and what others can do for them.

Emotional Bully – A toxic friend who intimidates you by using verbally and/or emotionally abusive tactics in order to control or manipulate you.

Emotional Manipulators – Category of toxic friends who like to play unfriendly mind games that cause a lot of emotional pain and suffering for the victim.

Empathy – The ability to understand someone else's feelings and difficulties, to walk in their shoes, and to see things from their perspective.

Envious – Extremely jealous toxic friend who dislikes you because of what you have or have accomplished.

Exposer – Toxic friend who discloses your secrets and confidences and tells your personal business to others by either gossiping or spreading rumors about you.

Extremists – Category of toxic friends who exaggerate every aspect of their life to the point of irritation, frustration, and disgust for those who are involved with them.

Fault Finders – Category of toxic friends who blame you for all the shortcomings or negativity in their life.

Flunky – Toxic friend who acts as a servant to many and does whatever anyone tells her to do.

Former Toxic Friend (FTF) – A toxic friend who has been successfully removed from your life.

Friendship Privileges – Special advantages, immunity, rights, permission, or benefits granted to a friend that gives her a high status or rank on your friendship list and are usually only given to a close or best friend.

Friend versus Frienemy Test – Test used to help you determine whether your friend is a *true* friend or a frienemy.

Frienemy – The friend you love and hate at the same time; she's your best friend but also your worst enemy as well.

Frienemy-ship – The unhealthy relationship, connection, or bond one develops with a frienemy.

FTF – Acronym for *former toxic friend*.

Games of Deception – Games designed to subtly deceive you in one way or another.

Gas Lighter – Toxic friend who is a psychological abuser that tries to systematically control you, drive you insane, and screw up your perception of reality.

Grouch – A habitually mean and nasty toxic friend who is always in a bad mood and/or angry all the time.

Guilt Tripper – Toxic friend who tries to make you feel guilty about everything you do or say.

Heartbreakers – Category of toxic friends who cause deep emotional hurt, pain, and sadness.

Hetero-Flexible – Toxic friend who identifies herself as heterosexual but is not afraid to explore her curiosity towards the same sex.

Houdini – A very clever toxic friend who has mastered the craft of escaping accountability, responsibility, conflict, and/or confusion.

Indirect Questioning – These types of questions are longer forms of normal questions.

Injustice Collector – A grudge holder who remembers and itemizes every slight, real or imagined, and throws it back in your face repeatedly.

Interloper – Toxic friend who selfishly interferes with every aspect of your life without regards to any set boundaries.

Interrogator – Very nosey toxic friend who asks too many personal questions and always wants to know your business.

Intimacy – The non-sexual closeness of the relationship you have with your friend.

Intuition – A feeling, hunch, inkling, or suspicion that something is not right.

Jekyll & Hyde – Toxic friend who has unpredictable mood swings and can be nice one minute, then nasty the next.

JOT – Acronym for Journal of Toxicity *(see Journal of Toxicity)*.

Journal of Toxicity (JOT) – A journal used for documenting your experiences with a toxic friend.

Keeper – Toxic friend who constantly borrows your possessions or money and never returns them or pays you back.

Know-It-All – Toxic friend who thinks she's an expert on everything and tries to undermine your intelligence.

Learned Behavior – A behavior that someone observed or was taught and found to be beneficial to them in one way or another despite the negative effects the behavior may have on others.

Leeches – Category of toxic friends who are mental, physical, and financial freeloaders who exploit others in any way they can.

Level of Intimacy – Determines the status of your friendship with others; the higher the level of intimacy, the closer the friendship *(see Intimacy)*.

Liar – Toxic friend who finds it difficult to tell the truth, and therefore lies to you constantly.

Line of No Return – When your friend crosses a boundary line for the last and final time.

Lonely – Toxic friend who is overly dependent on your companionship and tries to use you as a cure-all for her loneliness.

Mind Game – Psychological trick used to manipulate and gain an advantage over someone.

Mind Sweeping – The process of cleansing one's mind and physical environment of all the tangible reminders of a toxic friendship, and it can be done by returning, trashing, storing, selling, or donating the items.

Misery Magnet – Sad and miserable toxic friend who tries to make you and everyone around her feel the same way that she does.

Narcissist – Toxic friend who is in love with herself and has no care or concern for others because she consumes all of her time and energy thinking about ways she can preserve her inflated sense of self.

Narcissistic Personality Disorder – This is a personality disorder characterized by extreme self-centeredness and arrogance. Persons with this disorder lack empathy and think they are better than others.

Needy – Toxic friend who is always in need of something and is very clingy and overly dependent on you.

Obnoxious – Toxic friend who behaves abhorrently and is very offensive and unpleasant to be around.

One Upper – Toxic friend who is always trying to be one up on you. If you've done something, she's done it ten times better than you.

Passive Aggressive – Toxic friend who uses non-verbal actions to let you know she's angry or upset.

Penny Pincher – Very cheap and thrifty toxic friend who doesn't like to spend her own money, but will gladly have you spend yours on her wants and needs.

People Pleaser – Over-indulging toxic friend who is on a never-ending mission to try and please others while neglecting herself.

Perpetrator – Toxic friend who treats you more like an enemy than a friend.

Personality Disorder – A personality disorder is a pattern of deviant or abnormal behavior that interferes with an individual's ability to maintain a healthy emotional state of mind as well as healthy interpersonal relationships with others.

Phony – Toxic friend who constantly pretends to be someone or something she's not.

Problem Solver – Toxic friend who is obsessed with solving your problems for you while ignoring her own.

Procrastinator – Toxic friend who perpetually postpones doing things in a timely manner.

Promiscuous – Toxic friend who is considered "loose" and sexually immoral.

Promise Breaker – Extremely unreliable and undependable toxic friend who constantly breaks promises.

Queen Bee – Bitchy toxic friend who acts like a Prima Donna and thinks she's better than everyone else.

Reality Check – Words and/or phrases used to help you see the truth about any given situation.

Rebound Friend – A newly acquired friend used just for the purpose of pacifying the loneliness and emptiness one feels when she breaks up with a close friend.

Red Flag – Negative, inappropriate, or unacceptable behavior that warns us of the impending toxicity of a friendship.

Regulator – Very bossy and demanding toxic friend who tries to control you and the friendship.

Religious Hypocrite – Toxic friend who thinks she's holier than thou and more faithful than you, but her actual behavior says otherwise.

Rescuers – Category of toxic friends who are addicted to saving you from all the things they feel you are incapable of handling yourself.

Rider – Toxic friend who graciously and often inconspicuously rides the coattails of others and likes to reap the benefits from others' success.

Runner – Toxic friend who is constantly on the run from the truth, responsibility, confrontation, and commitment.

Second Significant Other – This a friend with whom one has a very close emotional bond, which makes the relationship with her almost as important, if not as important, as the relationship with one's significant other.

Self-Centered – Selfish toxic friend who is only concerned with her own feelings, wants, needs, and desires and not yours or anyone else's.

Simpletons – Category of toxic friends who often lack common sense along with the inability to say "No."

Simulated Survivor – Survivor who chooses to remain in her toxic friendship but develops effective ways of dealing with the perpetrator.

Sitting Duck – Toxic friend who is constantly victimized by others for various reasons and is often the target of ridicule or harassment.

Sloth – Extremely lazy toxic friend who always expects others to do things that she should be doing for herself.

Snubber – Toxic friend who dislikes you and blatantly shuns or rejects you in front of others.

Spoiled Brat – Toxic friend who is a very selfish and demanding prima donna and expects you to cater to her every want and need, and be available at her beck and call.

Stalker – Toxic friend who invades your personal space without your permission and after you've indicated your desire for her to leave you alone.

Swindler – Toxic friend who steals from you by subtle deception, scams, devious schemes, or friendly fraud.

Talk-a-Holic – This is a toxic friend who talks constantly and excessively about anything and everything, but mostly about things that are irrelevant and unimportant.

Time Bandit – This is a toxic friend who likes to waste your personal time by wanting you to be available at her beck and call.

Toxic Best Friend – There is a strong emotional bond with this friend; she's a step above a close friend and has all the friendship benefits and privileges that one can offer to their best friend.

Toxic by Association – The tendency for one to become toxic or to exhibit such behaviors as a result of spending too much time with a toxic friend.

Toxic Casual Friend – There are no emotional bonds, friendship benefits, or privileges; you can take her or leave her.

Toxic Close Friend – This friend is step above the Casual Toxic Friend and there is an emerging emotional bond. However, due to the numerous exhibitions of toxic behaviors, she has yet to cross the line of becoming your Best Toxic Friend.

Toxic Connection – A toxic connection is an unhealthy relationship between two or more people.

Toxic Enabler – The victim who helps perpetuate the negative behaviors of their toxic friend.

Toxic Friend – A toxic friend is an unhealthy companion, who causes a lot of stress, strain, and unnecessary drama in your life.

Toxic Friendship – An unhealthy connection or relationship with a friend.

Toxic Friendship Project – Project developed to help bring global awareness to the phenomenon of toxic friendships.

Toxic Friendship Survey – Survey designed for the sole purpose of gathering information and data about toxic friendships.

Toxic Friendship Survivor – A toxic friendship survivor is someone who has successfully ended a toxic friendship and moved on with her life or someone who remains in a toxic friendship but develops effective ways of dealing with the perpetrator.

Toxic Friendship Test – Test used to confirm or deny one's suspicion of having a toxic friendship.

Toxic Stronghold – Anything that keeps one trapped in the bondage and confines of a toxic friendship.

True Survivor – Survivor who has successfully ended a toxic friendship and moved on with her life.

Unhealthy Friendship – A friendship that is harmful to one's mental, emotional, physical, physiological, financial, or spiritual well-being.

User – Toxic friend who uses you for her own personal gains.

Victimized – Toxic friend who believes others are out to get her and blames everyone, except self, for the bad things that happen in her life.

Whiner – Constantly whines and complains about everything using a very high pitched and irritating voice.

Xenophobic – Toxic friend who has extreme dislike or fear of that which is unknown or different from oneself.

Zombie – A mindless people-pleasing toxic friend who doesn't speak up for herself and allows others to run over her or take advantage of her.

To order additional copies of this book:
Please visit the Toxic Friendship Project at:
www.toxicfriendships.org

About the Author

Loraine Smith-Hines is a toxic friendship survivor and the founder of *The Toxic Friendship Project*, an organization which creates educational materials that teach others about the differences between healthy and unhealthy friendships. She is an educator, wife, and mother of three children. She currently resides in the Midwest.